Reading Papyri, Writing Ancient History

The ancient Mediterranean world brought to us by Herodotus, Thucydides, and Tacitus is one of politics, war, and the power elite of Greece and Rome. There was another ancient world, in which ordinary people made a living, sold land, ran their towns, and sued one another. This is the world that the papyri bring to life; this book is about how they do so.

Reading Papyri, Writing Ancient History demonstrates how historians can put together information from scattered and often badly damaged documents to build up a picture of the society, economy, and culture of the multicultural and multilingual world of antiquity. Through discussion of contemporary historical work on the documents, Roger Bagnall scrutinizes alternative ways of approaching these sources. He shows how the ancient historian can use the methodologies of anthropology, comparative history, and statistics alongside more traditional tools to turn these texts into questions and answers.

Students and teachers of ancient history will find *Reading Papyri, Writing Ancient History* an indispensable guide to using these ancient texts in their own work.

Roger S. Bagnall is Professor of Classics and History at Columbia University. His other publications include *Egypt in Late Antiquity* (1993) and *The Demography of Roman Egypt* (1994).

Approaching the Ancient World
Series editor: Richard Stoneman

The sources for the study of the Greek and Roman world are diffuse, diverse, and often complex, and special training is needed in order to use them to the best advantage in constructing a historical picture. The books in this series provide an introduction to the problems and methods involved in the study of ancient history. The topics covered will range from the use of literary sources for Greek history and for Roman history, through numismatics, epigraphy, and dirt archaeology, to the use of legal evidence and of art and artefacts in chronology. There will also be books on statistical and comparative method, and on feminist approaches.

The Uses of Greek Mythology
Ken Dowden

Art, Artefacts, and Chronology in Classical Archaeology
William R. Biers

Reading Papyri, Writing Ancient History
Roger S. Bagnall

Ancient History from Coins
Christopher Howgego

Reading Papyri, Writing Ancient History

Roger S. Bagnall

London and New York

First published 1995
by Routledge
11 New Fetter Lane, London EC4P 4EE

Simultaneously published in the USA and Canada
by Routledge
29 West 35th Street, New York, NY 10001

© 1995 Roger S. Bagnall

Typeset in Baskerville by
Ponting–Green Publishing Services, Chesham, Bucks
Printed and bound in Great Britain by
T.J. Press (Padstow) Ltd, Padstow, Cornwall

Every attempt has been made to seek copyright permission
for the figures and tables used in this book.
Copyright holders should contact Routledge, London,
with any queries.

British Library Cataloguing in Publication Data
A catalogue record for this book is available from the
British Library

Library of Congress Cataloguing in Publication Data
A catalogue record for this book has been requested

ISBN   0–415–09376–7
ISBN   0–415–09377–5 (pbk)

Contents

Plates

1 A letter from the archive of Zenon, written across the fibers along the height of a strip cut from a papyrus roll. *P. Col. Zen.* 19, 257 BC. Photograph courtesy of Rare Book and Manuscript Library, Columbia University Libraries.

2 A letter from the archive of Zenon, written with a rush rather than a reed pen (cf. W. Clarysse, "Egyptian Scribes Writing Greek," *Chronique d'Égypte* 68 [1993] 186–201). *P. Col. Zen.* 52, about 251 BC. Photograph courtesy of Rare Book and Manuscript Library, Columbia University Libraries.

3 Loan of grain in Demotic, with a seal, dated to the rebel pharaoh Ankhonnophris. *P. BM* IV (Andrews) 19 (EA inv. 10831), 194 BC. Photograph courtesy of the Trustees of the British Museum.

4 Deed of gift in Greek (inner text) with signatures in Aramaic and Nabataean on verso. H. Cotton, "The Archive of Salome Komaïse Daughter of Levi: Another archive from the 'Cave of the Letters,'" *ZPE* 105 (1995) 171–208, AD 129. Photograph by courtesy of the Israel Antiquities Authority.

5 A village secretary practices his signature. *P. Petaus* 121 (P. Köln inv. 328), *c.* AD 184. Photograph courtesy of Institut für Altertumskunde, Universität zu Köln.

6 Tablet from Vindolanda with letter of Chrauttius to Veldeius in Latin. Tab. Vindol. II 310 (inv. 86/470), *c.* AD 110. Photograph by Alison Rutherford, © University of Newcastle upon Tyne and The Vindolanda Trust.

7 Lease of land in the form of a notarial contract with signatures. *SB* VIII 9876 (P. Vindob. inv. G 25870), AD 534. Photograph courtesy of Papyrussammlung, Österreichische Nationalbibliothek.

8 Coptic ostrakon from the Monastery of Epiphanius: Letter concerning readmission of a person to communion, seventh century AD (cf. *Monastery of Epiphanius at Thebes* I 173 n. 5, 236 n. 1). Columbia Papyrus Collection, ostrakon inv. 24.6.4. Photograph courtesy of Rare Book and Manuscript Library, Columbia University Libraries.

Preface

Papyrology has tended to be one of the most resolutely technical and positivistic disciplines of antiquity. This characteristic has justifiable roots in the enormous investment of time and expertise, in palaeography and philology, that is necessary for reading and interpreting the texts, often preserved only fragmentarily and in difficult handwritings. Many papyrologists do not seek to go beyond reading, translating, and commenting on unpublished papyri, or improving the texts of those already published. But ever since the late nineteenth century, from the foundational work of Ulrich Wilcken, some scholars in the field have sought to use the papyri for broader historical work. The most obvious uses have involved papyri that helped define a traditional narrative of events, even if only from a "worm's-eye view,"[1] but there is now a century's tradition of work on social and economic history, which is hardly a new fashion in papyrology. Because the papyri are by far our best ancient source for many aspects of these areas of history, this historical work is vital to understanding the ancient world as a whole.

Outsiders are, however, often struck not by the breadth of application of the papyri but rather by the enclosed character of papyrology and the tendency of many papyrologists not to venture beyond what they construe as the bounds of the discipline; nor are many outsiders prepared to undertake the technical preparation necessary to meet the texts on their own terms.[2] This closed environment has, I believe, fostered a generally rather unreflective climate, in which the usability and uses of the evidence of the documents are taken for granted, and in which the really difficult questions about how far one may generalize from them are barely mentioned, let alone discussed explicitly. Methodological discourse in papyrology has been limited essentially to the editing and criticism of texts.[3] Two forces have pushed me toward such an explicit discussion in the last few years. The first was the writing of *Egypt in Late Antiquity*, which was begun in the late 1980s and finished in 1992. In this book the papyri play the central role, although I tried as far as I could to integrate their witness with other types of evidence. I found myself gradually pushed to think about the problems of the character of this evidence and what limits needed to be observed in generalizing from it. That experience led to the second impetus, a small conference on "Documenting Cultures: Written and Unwritten in Ancient Societies," which brought together papyrologists, archaeologists, anthropologists, and literary scholars, working in fields ranging from ancient Mesopotamia to contemporary Morocco, to talk about how they confront the silences of the documentary record.[4] In particular, this group of about twenty people talked about how far what does exist can be used to help reconstruct what does not and what alternative routes toward this reconstruction are fruitful.

These two experiences made Routledge's invitation to contribute a book on the papyri to this series attractive. The process of thinking about what I might say was a rewarding one, but it led me above all to realize that this book is, for me at least, only a start. I hope that it will encourage a wider discussion about some of the problems it raises, and I look forward to learning from that conversation.

In the course of writing this book I have as usual incurred many debts of gratitude. Most of these are to colleagues who have offered observations or references to useful works. But I am particularly indebted to the University of Helsinki for an invitation to lecture in May 1994, when I was able to present some of the ideas set out in the book; Maarit Kaimio and her colleagues made this an extremely pleasant experience. The writing of the book in the summer of that year was supported by a summer stipend from the National Endowment for the Humanities.

Various drafts of the book were read both by students and by colleagues. Of the latter I am particularly indebted for suggestions to Alan Bowman, Dirk Obbink, Leslie MacCoull, and Bruce Nielsen. My mother also helped eliminate a considerable number of unclear or ungainly passages. My thanks to all.

January, 1995

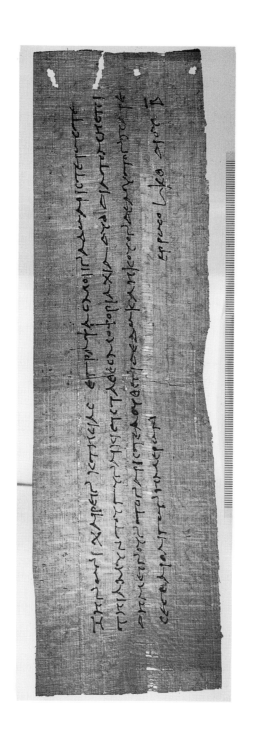

Figure 1 A letter from the archive of Zenon, written across the fibers along the height of a strip cut from a papyrus roll. *P.Col.Zen.* 19, 257 BC.

Figure 2 A letter from the archive of Zenon, written with a rush rather than a reed pen (cf. W. Clarysse, "Egyptian Scribes Writing Greek," *Chronique d'Égypte* 68 [1993] 186–201). *P.Col.Zen.* 52, about 251 BC.

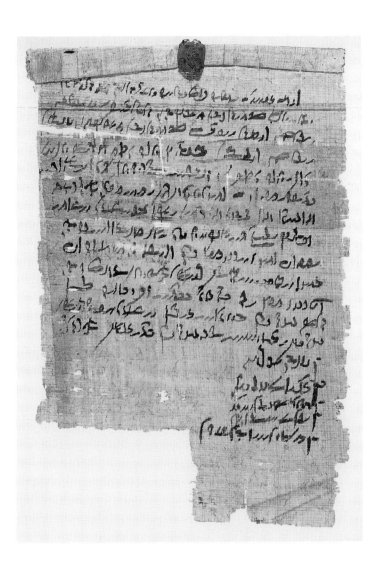

Figure 3 Loan of grain in Demotic, with a seal, dated to the rebel pharaoh Ankhonnophris. *P.BM* IV (Andrews) 19 (EA inv. 10831), 194 BC.

Figure 4 Deed of gift in Greek (inner text) with signature in Aramaic
and Nabataean on verso. H. Cotton, "The Archive of Salome Komaïse
Daughter of Levi: Another archive from the 'Cave of the Letters,'"
ZPE 105 (1995) 171–208, AD 129.

Figure 5 A village secretary practices his signature. *P. Petaus* 121 (P. Köln inv. 328), *c.* AD 184.

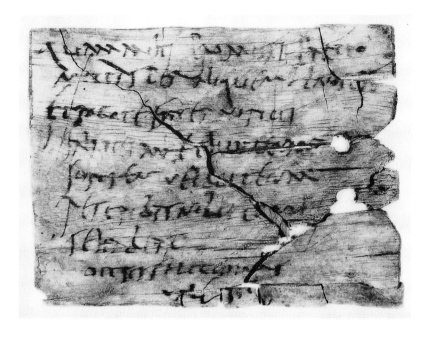

Figure 6 Tablet from Vindolanda with letter of Chrauttius to Veldeius in Latin. Tab. Vindol. II 310 (inv. 86/470), *c.* AD 110.

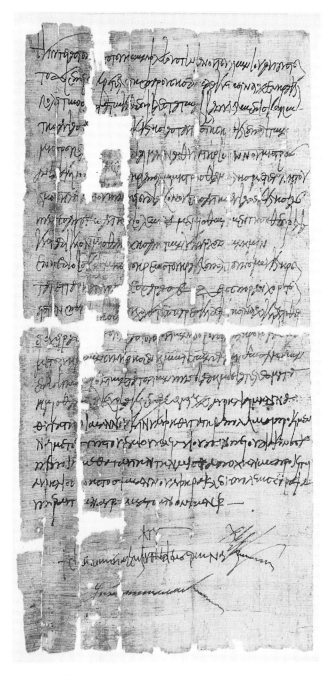

Figure 7 Lease of land in the form of a notarial contract with signatures.
SB VIII 9876 (P. Vindob.inv. G25870), AD 534.

Figure 8 Coptic ostrakon from the Monastery of Epiphanius: Letter concerning readmission of a person to communion, seventh century AD (cf. *Monastery of Epiphanius at Thebes* I 173 n. 5, 236 n. 1). Columbia Papyrus Collection, ostrakon inv. 24.6.4.

Introduction
History and Papyri

This book is concerned with the theory and method of using a particular body of ancient documents, the papyri, in the writing of history. Chapters 1 and 2 discuss papyrus as a writing material, describe other materials that fulfilled a similar purpose and are usually classed with the papyri, and ask where papyri come from and what sorts of texts they contain. But before we turn even to such basic questions as those, a yet more fundamental and daunting subject lies before us: What does writing history mean? This question is all the more inescapable because, as we shall see time and again, the papyri are not a particular closed world, and we cannot responsibly write history using them in isolation from other types of evidence, models, and questions. Nor, for that matter, are most of the characteristics of the papyri unique to them. No other body of evidence has quite the same configuration of features, perhaps, but to a considerable degree the problems facing the historian in the papyri are similar to those presented by the documents from Cairo's medieval Jewish community, preserved in the so-called "Cairo Geniza," to give just one example.[1]

Papyrology has, as I remarked in the preface, not been a very reflective discipline. Apart from a small body of work on editorial method, there are only occasional pieces, mostly talks given at congresses and many of them far narrower than their titles would suggest.[2] The reasons for this state of affairs probably lie mainly in the enormous technical demands of the discipline. Although papyrology is, from the point of view of research tools, a well-organized and provided field, it demands of its practitioners a tremendous investment of time in mastering palaeography, languages, editorial technique, and a specialized body of detailed information about institutions. Only a minority of those who work with the papyri have the combination of energy and interest to go beyond the work of editing and criticizing texts to that of using them for wider historical investigation, and hardly any of these have then taken the further measure of stepping outside the role of historian to look at the character of the enterprise itself. This absence of methodological discussion is not the result of any principled belief in a pure documentary empiricism, which is by now truly a straw man in professional debate. Rather, it is the outcome of a lack of reflection bred of the technical demands mentioned above and perhaps a conviction that theoretical discussion does not really lead to any result.

The same technical hurdles have formed an almost insuperable barrier to use of the papyri by historians not trained in papyrology.[3] The risk of making serious errors in using the papyri is greatly enlarged for those who cannot control the texts they use, for these texts often contain errors of reading and restoration. It is almost impossible to check every detail of every text for any subject, of course, but a combination of deep familiarity with the papyri, their language, and their contents, coupled with palaeographical skill, can allow – indeed, virtually require – the historian to correct numerous texts along the way to almost any historical synthesis. Any historian unable to do this competently is likely to build on sand. Some historians have dealt with a bad conscience brought on by ignoring the papyri through rationalizations that Egypt was a world apart and can be left out of account.[4] We shall see repeatedly that this view is bankrupt.[5]

Now it is a commonplace – especially among social scientists – that historians are unreceptive to, even hostile to, theory. Papyrological lack of reflection may therefore seem nothing more than a case of the ordinary. But this may be going too far. Theory, after all, is a term with multiple meanings that need to be disentangled. "Like so many words that are bandied about, the word theory threatens to become meaningless. Because its referents are so diverse – including everything from minor working hypotheses, through comprehensive but vague and unordered speculations, to axiomatic systems of thought – use of the word often obscures rather than creates understanding."[6]

One of these meanings is "some kind of general system of explanation,"[7] essentially what is sometimes called the substantive philosophy of history. Such philosophies or theories, such master explanations, generally originate outside the study of history. Philosophy, politics, and religion have all provided such general keys to the meaning of history. Probably the most influential of these in the twentieth century has been Marxism, but if one looks back over the last three centuries it is only one of numerous claimants. In ancient history, the work and approach of Max Weber has been at least as influential, in considerable part because of its centrality in the writings of Moses Finley.[8]

Historians are undoubtedly more hostile to theories of the master-explanation type than to any other, and with reason. There is a cogent philosophical argument, which I accept, that such substantive philosophy of history is inherently "a misconceived activity," essentially because our "knowledge of the past is significantly limited by our ignorance of the future."[9] This sort of theory will therefore largely be left out of account here. This may seem rather cavalier; in its defense I can say only that no good purpose would be served by using my limited space in rehashing an argument that in my view has already been made decisively. These large-scale explanations do, to my mind, have some use if deployed only as models to stimulate thinking and as sources of questions, but none at all when treated like historical laws.[10]

One particular flavor of general theory deserves comment before we pass on, however. The reader of historical studies based on the papyri may occasionally be tempted to think that papyrologists are, even if they do not acknowledge it, historical materialists. That is, even if not pure Marxists, they may give primacy to material factors in constructing historical explanations, somewhat like the earlier generations of historians in the French *Annales* school.[11] It is, of course, possible that this is true of some individual scholars, but the concentration of papyrological history on materialist questions is primarily the product of the surviving documentation itself, which generally created in order to record – even embody – material rights and obligations and, most particularly, to allow the government to exercise control over the population. The bias in the documents produced by this factor is discussed in chapter 2. It is fair to say that scholars have not always been as conscious of the dangers posed for their work by this bias as they might be. It is also true that the physical character of Egypt has a profound and visible effect on its life, one by which historians have been profoundly marked; the Nile's flood was not socially constructed (although it has now been socially destroyed by the High Dam at Aswan!). All the same, it would be a mistake to elevate scholarly unreflectiveness into any systematic materialist philosophical viewpoint.

Much, perhaps most, of what is generally called theory is of a less ambitious cast, "theories of the middle range." These are

> theories that lie between the minor but necessary working hypotheses that evolve in abundance during day-to-day research and the all-inclusive systematic efforts to develop a unified theory that will explain all the observed uniformities of social behavior, social organization and social change.[12]

Indeed, a recent book on the uses of social theory in historical scholarship is mainly devoted to sections on "central concepts" and "central problems."[13] Whether the word "theory" is necessarily aptly used with reference to concepts like class, power, social movements, status, patronage, corruption, and the like seems to me doubtful, but for particular theorists these terms certainly have conveyed much more specific senses than historians usually give them – at least consciously – and thus express underlying theories. Much of this middle-range theory, in effect the conceptual equipment with which we study the evidence of antiquity, is at stake in chapters 3–7 of this book.

Theory may also refer to views about the act of writing history, particularly about the proper methods for this work and the kinds of interests that the historian should pursue. All historians, even papyrological ones, have in this sense some sort of theoretical foundation for their work, however implicit it may be. Choices of this sort, after all, must be made, for history is not about the reproduction of the past but about its organization and understanding.[14] This is no less true – in fact it is more than ever true – when one is dealing with original documents from antiquity, which are in one obvious sense "closer" to the past. As Marc Bloch put it, to "venture to recount all these activities without selection and rearrangement

. . . would be to sacrifice clarity, not to the true order of reality – which is composed of natural affinities and underlying connections – but to the purely superficial order of contemporaneousness."[15]

The making of choices about selection, organization, questions, methods, and presentation opens up a great variety of possibilities for the historian. It has also fueled an extensive debate over the last century about the inherent difficulty of looking at history as an "objective" discipline. The impact of postmodernist criticism has undermined still further the confidence in scientific, objective history prevalent in the nineteenth century. Discussion of these issues has at times reached a pitch of vociferousness[16] and confusion, with whole regiments of straw men arrayed for battle, that must leave most outsiders perplexed. It is impossible to give here even a sketch of this subject; but there are signs among historians of a developing consensus, which may be stated in oversimplified form as follows: The choice of approaches and subjects in writing history is profoundly subjective and molded by the opportunities, pressures, and passions of the historian's time and background. Within any particular investigation, however, it is possible to make statements that demonstrably approach the truth, however imperfect their formulation by any given scholar, and these statements can be discussed by commonly agreed-upon criteria and methods.[17] This viewpoint allows historians to be acutely aware of their limitations and those of their craft without allowing these to paralyze them.[18] In fact, it affirms and celebrates the diversity of gifts that historians bring to their task; the writing of history would be much impoverished if all historians had the same range of strengths.

Such an approach differs importantly from much writing about the nature of history, both by historians and by philosophers, in rejecting the prescriptive character that many such works adopt. The work of definition, by its nature, is engaged in exclusion. Definitions allow some types of work to be called history, others not to be; in fact, that is their purpose. Even philosophers who avowedly start from a descriptive standpoint, talking about what they observe historians doing, tend to work toward such a prescriptive result.[19] The same tendency can sometimes be observed in historians who are apostles of particular types of historical research. Few nowadays are so naive as to assert that theirs is the only valid approach, but their own method still tends to derive its validity in opposition to others, in a kind of pragmatic polemics.[20] This stance is untenable if history is truly open, if the future continues to transform it.[21] Future events will both force us to make different statements about past events, by changing the results, fulfillment, or nullification of those past events, and also bring new tools and approaches, which we cannot even imagine today, but which will have much to contribute to the understanding of the past. A single example will make the point sufficiently. Suppose that Ulrich Wilcken, in the early 1880s, had possessed the 300 census declarations from Roman Egypt that we now have, instead of the two dozen or so that he did. He could certainly then have read his texts far better than he actually did. But he could not have derived from them what we can today,[22] because the modern science of demography simply did not exist. The comparative data, the mathematical models, the life tables, and the computerized tools of analysis all readily available today were not even imagined. Only an extraordinary solipsism would deny the certainty that such revolutions will continue to occur into the indefinite future.

It follows that the repertory of valuable approaches is open-ended, and that we cannot even be confident that we know where they all fit within an overall architecture of history. An approach based on definition and exclusion is not viable. As Fernand Braudel put it, "I would claim . . . that all doors seem to me good when crossing the multiple threshold of history."[23] Similarly, an attempt to draw the lines of disciplines in any clear fashion is unworkable. It is not worth the effort to lay down stern rules about where the distinction between history and anthropology lies, for example.[24] No scholar today can be unaware of the degree to which disciplinary boundaries have been eroded, or of the constant turmoil in disciplinary identity that has resulted. But this need not be seen as a crisis, or even as worrisome.

The theoretical framework of the following chapters, therefore, reflects this inclusive, open, multidimensional approach to methods. It will be exemplified by the deployment of examples of various methods and styles of investigation. In each case I shall attempt to give the gist of the argument presented by the scholar or scholars responsible for it, and look at this for evidence of methodological notions, whether explicit or implicit. It has seemed to me most useful to choose almost entirely positive examples rather than negative – that is, to present instances that I regard as good work. In part, this makes for a more agreeable and less carping flow of discussion, but it also has a positive didactic purpose in line with the inclusive rather than exclusive approach defended above. This does not, however, mean that I do not criticize what seem to me to be weak points in the arguments or elucidate points of method that modify or limit the conclusions of the book or article in question. In many cases I do so, precisely to indicate again the openness to further consideration of both methodological and substantive conclusions. For the most part the examples presented come from fairly recent work and, with a few exceptions, from scholars I know or have known. Although these represent diverse approaches and schools of thought, this is still only a sampler, which inevitably reflects my own interests and biases. It is not any sort of comprehensive roster of "good" work, and it is *certainly* not intended to imply any negative judgment about works not mentioned.

One recurrent theme of the book deserves to be signalled here. This is its emphasis on the interactive, recursive character of the twin operations of forming and testing hypotheses. It is my conviction that these are the essential intellectual activities of historical investigation, and that they are in character not greatly different from the workings of most scientific research. In a logical sense the formation of hypotheses (abduction, in Peircean terminology) precedes the testing of them by deducing their consequences and seeing if the evidence can disprove the supposed results of the hypothesis. But in actual operation, the relationship of these activities is not so neatly distinguishable, and one feeds another constantly. I have in fact put chapters mainly devoted to the analysis of evidence first, those devoted to the formation of questions and hypotheses second, in order to avoid making matters too neat. This is not because I accept the simplistic logic of statements like this dictum of Le Roy Ladurie: "On the contrary, the theory simply leaps out of the overwhelming evidence."[25] But neither is it true, as François Furet once claimed, that "it is not the sources which define the questions asked by a discipline, but the questions which determine the sources."[26] Despite the theoretical sequence here from evidentiary analysis (the basis of testing hypotheses) to the asking of questions (the mother of hypotheses), then, my emphasis throughout will be on the way in which both are constantly in process as the historian works.

Chapter 1

The culture of papyrus

The Introduction has provided a brief sketch of what I suppose to be involved in writing history, and particularly in writing history of the ancient world, taking account of broader currents of thought about the nature of the historical enterprise at the end of the twentieth century. We turn now to the other element of our subject, the papyri themselves. Understanding what papyri are, where they come from, and who used them in antiquity for what purpose is central to knowing how we can in our turn use those papyri that have survived in our search for understanding the ancient world. Indeed, the answers to such questions direct and limit our historical inquiries in ways both obvious and subtle. Much of the rest of this book is devoted to exploring such complexities. This chapter can, however, make no attempt to be a general manual of papyrology, nor even a précis of one. Such works exist and serve their purposes well; replacing them is not our purpose here.[1] Rather, we will be concerned with the few specific questions mentioned above. This initial discussion will take in the broad geographical range encompassed by the surviving documents and place these questions in a general frame of reference. Chapter 2 then focuses in more detail on Egypt and on several aspects of the textual material that have a sharp and immediate impact on the existing documentation.

The term "papyrus" here is to be taken throughout this book to represent a class of written artefacts, not all actually involving papyrus as a material. The ancient societies that used papyrus also used pieces of broken pottery (called ostraka), parchment, wooden tablets and labels, and bone for the same kinds of purposes for which papyrus was employed. What these materials generally have in common is that they were used for written artefacts with no particular pretensions to permanence. The *texts* written on these materials might or might not have been thought of by their authors as possessions for all time; we may imagine that most authors of what we call literature shared Thucydides' hopes. But the particular embodiment of a text on a physical medium was endowed with no such expectations. When greater permanence was the goal, the ancients used stone or sometimes metal (generally bronze) and usually cut or cast the letters into the material rather than writing them with ink. Such inscriptions generally had a purpose of public display, also distinguishing them from most (though not all) texts on papyrus and the materials we assimilate to papyrus.

Papyri (in this broader sense) have survived from antiquity to the present in a radically uneven pattern. This pattern may be regarded as reflecting the operation of two variables, climate and ancient patterns of usage. The first of these is relatively well understood, but the second is as yet little known. Papyrus, like any organic material (including ink, which was made with carbon black and gum arabic[2]), survives best when protected from air and water. In practice this means that ground water and rain are the principal enemies of papyrus, and that desert terrain is best suited to its preservation. Egypt's dry zones have been much the richest sources of finds of ancient organic material, but similar, though slightly less arid, zones exist in other parts of North Africa and the Near East.

There is thus in principle no reason why discoveries of papyri should not be made in these dry zones, and in fact the pace of such finds has been accelerating. We now have papyri in Greek, Latin, Hebrew, Aramaic, Syriac, and other languages from various parts of the Near East, including the Negev (Nessana), the Dead Sea region, the middle Euphrates valley (including Dura-Europos), and Arabia (Bostra and Petra).[3] Arabic papyri are known from Samarra and near Damascus.[4] Ostraka have been found in Libya (Bu Njem) and the Dead Sea (Masada).[5] It seems reasonable to expect that modern archaeological techniques will, if given the political conditions necessary to allow excavations throughout this complex region, continue to find new bodies of papyrological material.

On the north side of the Mediterranean, despite what usually seems to those from rainier climates like pervasive dryness, there is actually a fair amount of annual rainfall, and the same is much more true of northern Europe. In these areas the conditions are far less favorable for the survival of papyri, and unusual circumstances are generally required. Such circumstances do occur. Two notable examples are the preservation of papyri and stylus tablets from Herculaneum (and other settlements on the Bay of Naples) because of carbonization in the eruption of Vesuvius in AD 79, and the survival of wooden tablets written with ink in anaerobic bog-like conditions at Vindolanda in Britain.[6] Once again, there is every reason to think that more such discoveries will occur in expert excavations, though probably not with the frequency that may be hoped for in the Near East.[7]

Northern and western discoveries of documents have thus been mainly tablets and graffiti; the Herculaneum papyri were a private philosophical library.[8] Eastern and southern discoveries have been mainly papyri and ostraka. How far is this a matter of the circumstances of preservation, and how far one of ancient availability of or preference for particular materials? Neither factor can be entirely responsible, but the relative weights to be given are by no means obvious. Proximity to Egypt, the only source of actual papyrus, is unlikely to have been unimportant, and no doubt papyrus acquired a cost disadvantage with the interposition of distance from Egypt. Even within Egypt it may sometimes have been cheaper or handier to use tablets, as recent finds from the Dakleh Oasis in the western desert suggest. We shall return to this question a little later.

For the moment, however, two other points about the distribution of the finds deserve attention. First, despite the importance of what has turned up outside Egypt, the valley of the Nile is still the source of the overwhelming bulk of our papyrological documentation. That fact has perennially raised questions about how broadly the historian is permitted to use the papyri to describe conditions in other parts of the Hellenistic and Roman worlds, often referred to as the problem of typicality. How representative of the larger Greek and Roman world is the picture provided by the papyri? Was Egypt "normal" or a world of its own? It has often been difficult to separate this question from the self-interest of those answering it, whether by papyrologists in favor of typicality or by historians lacking expertise in the papyri (and, as papyrologists always suspect, averse to the effort of acquiring it) against typicality.[9] This issue poses itself in all sorts of ways. For example, how normal was Egypt in the range and quantity of written documents used? Most ancient historians have viewed it as an aberrant land of bureaucracy and papyrus,[10] but the recent finds ranging from Vindolanda to Petra have made this view increasingly untenable.

Even if the *existence* of extensive written documentation outside Egypt is admitted, however, one may ask how normal either the documentary practices or the institutions and society revealed by the papyri are. These questions are much harder, but recent work has tended to suggest that differences in documentary practices were relatively small, with a wide zone of commonality visible at least within the Greek-writing part of the Mediterranean.[11] More importantly, perhaps, the entire notion of normality deserves to be rethought: Was Egypt more different from other regions than they were from one another? Is there a Hellenistic or Roman "standard" against which regions can be measured?

The second point is related to the first. Egypt itself cannot be taken as a unitary whole without serious reservations. The papyri are not found in a kind of even scatter throughout that country, but come mainly from intense concentrations in a few places. Little has come from cities and villages with continuing habitation in the twentieth century, and very little from currently cultivated zones, where irrigation water has generally destroyed ancient organic material. Instead, the pattern of finds favors cemeteries, the edges of the desert, places that have dried up, and (particularly in the last decade) the deeper reaches of the desert. In some respects, this pattern is a survival of the least fit; the most fertile and continuously occupied lands of Egypt are documentarily blank.

Such a situation is not necessarily a major obstacle to historical investigation. In questions where there is no particular reason to suppose that locale plays a determinative role, a non-random sample of sources may not be much worse than a random one. In others, particularly where ecology, economy, and social habits interact, it may deprive us of large areas of knowledge. The single most important such blank for Egypt is the Nile's delta, where as many as two-thirds of the population may have lived in the Roman period, and where ecological conditions differed significantly from those in the narrow Nile valley further south. The implications of place in the historical analysis of the papyri will occupy a good part of the next two chapters.

Availability of writing materials and patterns of preservation and discovery may be thought of as a series of filters between the observer and the object of study. Another aspect of availability of papyrus also acts as such a filter, but in such a manner that it is also part of the image we study. The labor involved in making papyrus was considerable, and its price was therefore significant, most typically several days' average worker's wages for a roll.[12] In some places, wooden tablets (which could be reused more readily than could papyrus) were an economically advantageous substitute, but these too required precision tools and skilled labor to manufacture.[13] For members of the proper-tied classes, the cost was no deterrent, but for poor peasants it might be. Nor did their normal illiteracy render the availability of papyrus irrelevant to them, for they had to provide the material for receipts written by officials for the taxes they paid. In such cases, as when supply problems to distant points made papyrus scarce, broken pieces of pottery could be found every-where for the taking, and tens of thousands of them have survived with receipts, letters, lists, and accounts.

The economic cost of raw materials was, however, certainly not the only, nor even the major, determinant of who used papyrus. Nor was the ability to write and read. Rather, the prime motivator for use was *need* for written documentation. In principle, this need might be as great for an illiterate money-lender as for a literate one, for both participated in an economy dependent on writing and needed the security provided by the documents, which they could always have someone else write and read for them.

A very large part (though hardly all) of what was written existed in some sense to exercise someone's power over some-one else.[14] The largest consumer of papyrus was thus the government, which needed to keep records of people and property, compute, record, and transmit their taxes, keep track of its own expenditure, carry on a voluminous internal cor-respondence, and send to the ultimate authorities a report of all that had been done. For the government, the cost of papyrus was no doubt very large, but it was not material compared to the cost of the labor to produce, process, and store the documentation, let alone the total revenues and expenditures at stake. Cost was thus no object, and it is in public documentation that we witness the least parsimonious use of the material.

For individuals, the need for writing emerged above all for protecting property rights – recording ownership of land, houses, slaves, and animals; documenting obligations (or their satisfaction) in money or produce; and providing evidence that they had discharged their obligations of various sorts toward the government. Most such contracts were drawn up by professional scribes trained in contractual formulas, whose characteristic, stereotyped handwritings are instantly recognizable to the trained eye. The common trait of these transactions is their view toward the future, when a debt had to be collected, a would-be creditor repulsed, ownership defended, or claims by the government warded off. Duplicate (or even multiple) copies might be needed to protect the different interests of the parties.[15] Transactions with no future – I hand you a sack of radishes, you hand me a coin – generally needed no written record. Individuals did sometimes keep accounts of receipts and expenditures, but these are largely the product of wealthy individuals and families.[16]

There is no systematic census of published, much less of unpublished, papyri, but the categories of texts and their occasions enumerated in the last two paragraphs come close to representing perhaps 80 to 90 percent of the known papyri.[17] There are a few other groups of importance. One is the private letters, a body of material still largely unstudied as a source for social history.[18] Another is the corpus of hundreds of texts emanating from the process of education, at the elementary level both in letters and in numbers, and at the more advanced level in literature, rhetoric, and scribal practice.[19] Finally, of course, there are the literary papyri, ranging from private extracts from works to complete books produced according to the highest standards of luxury.

The corner of documentation occupied by the school texts and literary papyri is a privileged locus. Although the number of people who received a basic education in writing and reading was not small, it certainly remained a distinct minority of the population, drawn entirely from those groups able to afford both to pay for education – there was no free public education in most of the ancient world – and to dispense with their children's labor while they were learning.[20] This was at least as true of Demotic Egyptian, and later Coptic, as of Greek. How far the situation with Latin in the western provinces of the Roman empire, which lacked an antecedent tradition of writing, was different we are only beginning to be able to consider.[21] The use of literate abilities for something beyond the needs of daily life and business was certainly far more restricted than those practical uses, and in all periods the ownership and enjoyment of literature was the prerogative of the top stratum of society.

The culture of papyrus, then, was both embracing and restrictive. Hardly anyone, except infants who died before being recorded, would escape some involvement with the comprehensive network of private and governmental documentation, and even the poorest families were likely to own something written. But many people would have only a second-hand acquaintance with the world of writing, depending on others to write things for them where necessary and to keep them informed about things that affected them. The power of this second-hand relationship should not be underestimated, however, for it concerned aspects of life of vital importance to their physical and economic security or even survival. Equally importantly for our purposes, the close relationship of most writing to the economic and administrative spheres means both that they are overdocumented relative to their place in human activity generally and that those persons most involved in them are also overrepresented in the surviving record. This is the sense in which the social character of writing and its dependence on power act as another filter between our gaze and ancient society.

In another sense, however, this filter is defined by and helps to represent that society. In this respect it is very different from a filter like the choices of modern excavators. The great stratification of wealth, education, and power embedded in the pattern of the use of writing by the ancients is itself one of the key characteristics of ancient society. A pattern that impedes our understanding of some aspects of antiquity is thus a direct revelation of others. Both of these aspects will play a role in our assessment of the possibilities and limits of using papyri for historical study.

Chapter 2

Ancient and modern choices in documentation

In chapter 1 we saw something of the range of surviving papyrus documentation from around the Mediterranean world and even northern Europe. Despite the progress of recent decades, the finds outside Egypt are still patchy, scattered enough that the density of information available in Egypt is simply not present. Later chapters will refer to this non-Egyptian material occasionally, but the historian working with papyri is usually of necessity driven to think about methods and materials largely in the Egyptian context. In the present chapter, then, we will focus on four key determinants of the information available to us from the Egyptian papyri and how they form the indispensable base for the more detailed studies on the use of evidence in chapters 3–5. These are languages and scripts, types of documents and their mode of production, survival of texts, and the use of damaged documents.

LANGUAGES AND SCRIPTS

The linguistic world of the eastern Mediterranean in Hellenistic and Roman antiquity would in many ways have seemed familiar to many modern Europeans, but strange to most Americans. It witnessed the coexistence of one, then two international languages with a host of local ones. Greek may already have acquired something of an international status even before Alexander the Great, although Aramaic served as the standard means of communication in the polyglot Persian empire;[1] but after his conquests it was the unrivalled language of political power and interregional commerce for a thousand years. The Roman conquest provided an overlay of Latin in political and military affairs, but otherwise left the dominance of Greek untroubled, even in the documentary sphere for the most part.

Side by side with these international languages there survived and flourished a wide variety of local or regional languages, in a profusion of dialects. Many of these never achieved written form and are lost to us, but in both the Near East and Egypt there are extensive bodies of written material through most of the period from Alexander to the Arab conquests. In the case of Egypt, the native language had achieved written form long before Greek did, in the hieroglyphic script that fascinated ancient and modern observers. This script was not extinct in the Ptolemaic and Roman periods, although those trained to write it declined in numbers and their work became increasingly obscure to all but a handful. Still, there are numerous cases in the Ptolemaic period where inscriptions in hieroglyphic script, particularly grave stelai, intersect with documentation in Greek to provide indispensable evidence and a far richer picture. A remarkable example is the discovery that some members of a prominent family at Apollonopolis Magna (Edfu, in Upper Egypt) are commemorated by dual grave stelai. One is in Greek verse, uses Greek names, and displays Greek official titles. The other is in hieroglyphs, has traditional Egyptian names, and mentions Egyptian priestly offices in the local temple. As one scholar has put it, "the two aspects did not merge, but were kept separate like the two faces of a Janus-statue."2

By the Hellenistic period, the hieroglyphs had become essentially a specialized tool for temple inscriptions and grave stelai of important persons. The earliest more cursive derivative of this script, called "hieratic," although used in earlier periods for a broad range of purposes, had also now become specialized, again within the temple communities, for certain religious texts.3 For most other purposes, hieratic had in turn given way to a yet more cursive script referred to as "Demotic." Like its predecessors, Demotic was a complex script using alphabetic, syllabic, and ideographic characters, and its users were mainly professional scribes and other high-ranking officials of the administration and temples. It may in fact owe its origins to the need of the Saite dynasty for a linguistic tool for the reunification of Egypt.4 The famous Rosetta Stone, which opened the way to the decipherment of hieroglyphs nearly two centuries ago, had versions in Demotic and in Greek next to that in hieroglyphs. In the earlier Ptolemaic period Demotic held its own and had a literary efflorescence.[5]

In the early Roman period, however, Demotic began a swift and dramatic decline in both the private sphere, where contracts in the script become rare after the reign of Augustus, and the public, where the one remaining use, tax receipts on ostraka, falls off sharply after the Julio-Claudian period.[6] By the second half of the second century, Demotic had become what hieroglyphs were in the later Ptolemaic period, a learned survival holding out in a few enclaves but irrelevant to most people for daily purposes. This decline was probably in part the natural result of Greek dominance of political and economic life, but the sharp downturn in the Roman period may well have been affected by the Romans' lack of support for the temples, the natural home of the scripts, and perhaps (it has been argued) by their refusal of official recognition to contracts written in Egyptian.[7]

For much of the Roman period, then, there was no version of Egyptian in common use for ordinary writing purposes. In the third century this gap was filled. After centuries of experiments in writing the Egyptian language in Greek alphabetic characters, a new and coherent writing system was developed, which we call Coptic. The Coptic alphabet enriched the Greek with signs derived from Demotic in order to represent the phonology of Egyptian better than unaided Greek letters could, but the language also borrowed large numbers of words from Greek to enrich the Egyptian vocabulary. The result was a written embodiment of Egyptian with both simplicity and power. It was initially used for biblical texts, but by the middle of the fourth century the range had begun to expand to other Christian literary works and to private letters. The regional dialects of Egyptian, largely hidden from view by the formal character of Demotic, reemerged in Coptic, although the Sahidic and then Bohairic dialects eventually prevailed as literary languages.

It might seem unnecessary to point out that the historian concerned with Egypt in a particular period should take account of the evidence in all languages surviving from that period. And indeed this statement has become a commonplace in the literature of the last quarter-century. But prescriptions are still more common than examples, for the simple reason that Greek and Egyptian are normally part of very different (and already demanding) graduate programs and few scholars learn both well enough to do original work in them. Even those trained only in Greek still can make good use of Egyptian material, however, if they take the trouble. The most dramatic instance of such integration by a Hellenist is Dorothy Thompson's book on Ptolemaic Memphis.[8] The point of entry into the world of Memphis – an Egyptian royal capital for millennia – and its sanctuaries, for a classically trained historian, is the archive of Ptolemaios from the Sarapieion, one of the earliest bodies of Greek papyri to be published. But even a first reading of these papyri shows the impossibility of understanding them in isolation, for Ptolemaios spent the twenty years of his life which these papyri document inside an Egyptian sanctuary on the west bank of the Nile. Understanding the environment and Ptolemaios' activities is impossible without close study of the Egyptian milieu, which leads Thompson into Demotic and hieroglyphic sources, as well as the results of excavations of Memphis and its surroundings. As a result, the book's documentary foundation is very largely Egyptological rather than Greek, and the complex society of the Memphite region is seen from both Greek and Egyptian perspectives as far as the evidence allows.

The small group of scholars who have actually mastered both languages has also begun to have a major impact. An example is a study by P. W. Pestman showing that the notaries responsible for Greek contracts at Pathyris, all of them with Greek names, in fact had Egyptian names as well, wrote Demotic as well as Greek, and held military ranks.[9] Because the information connected by Pestman appears in texts in both languages, but not enough material to support the connections comes from either language separately, the entire phenomenon revealed by the study would have remained invisible without Pestman's control of both bodies of papyri. This case was then used by Willy Clarysse as part of a larger argument that a considerable number of people in Ptolemaic Egypt, particularly in the second and first centuries BC, operated with effective dual names and identities, which they used depending on the circumstances and the nature of the function being filled.[10] This discovery is an important element in the reshaping of views of ethnicity and culture in Ptolemaic Egypt in progress today. The lessons to be learned from such cases should not be oversimplified. Certainly the importance of bringing the material together is clear. But so also is the fundamental disjunction that made recognition of the connection so difficult. For the most part, Demotic texts tend to be very different from Greek texts and to fulfill different functions; they are not simply Greek papyri in Egyptian.[11] The classically trained reader at once recognizes substantial differences in approach and in modes of expression that give an air of strangeness to Demotic texts. Far fewer of them have so far been published than of Greek papyri, even for the periods where they coexist, and a thorough description of their differing territories would be premature. Demotic seems to have been far more used in the royal administration in the third century than the second, for example. Egyptians wishing to use their own law would produce contracts in Demotic, not Greek; but as time passed, they increasingly sought access to the Greek courts and used Greek documents with some sophistication.

The complex interplay of types of documentation can be seen in a protracted struggle between a family of Egyptian funerary priests and a Greek military officer over ownership of a house at Thebes, which resulted in a trial before royal officials – decisively won by the Egyptians. The dossier of this case, now elegantly reedited by Pestman, shows that the contracts pertinent to the house were mostly written in Egyptian, but the records of payment of transfer taxes, petitions to royal officials, and the protocol of the trial are all in Greek, and the advocate for the Egyptians has a Greek name.[12] All this suggests that the historian must pay considerable attention to questions of the use of the different languages for particular purposes and certainly not assume that they are in any sense equivalent.

The same is largely true for Coptic, though for rather different reasons. The dominance of Greek in official and economic matters was unchallenged for several centuries after the first appearance of Coptic. This is hardly surprising, for Coptic was developed in a bilingual milieu and by people who knew Greek well. The specifically Christian character of the early Coptic texts is notable, and it is not until the sixth century that the first legal texts in Coptic begin to appear.[13] Only after the Arab conquest did Coptic begin to fulfill the same functions as Greek and start to replace it, and from that point large numbers of texts like contracts and tax receipts start to be written. For this reason, Coptic is central to understanding Egyptian Christianity[14] but not, until the sixth and even more the seventh century, for many aspects of administrative, social, and economic life. For this later period, however, it is Greek that begins to be marginalized, and the historian must confront the two on an equal footing.

Before leaving languages and scripts, something must be said of those other than Greek and Egyptian. Only a tiny number – around 1 percent – of Latin texts have been found, proportionate to those in Greek, and these are restricted largely to military and official contexts, as well as situations involving Roman law in the earlier principate.[15] From the period of Persian rule in Egypt, a number of Aramaic papyri were found at Elephantine, at the first cataract of the Nile. These stem from the Jewish garrison stationed there in the fifth century BC. Aramaic is otherwise extremely rare in the papyri. When the Persians conquered Egypt again briefly in the early seventh century of our era, they left behind a certain number of papyri in their language; these are again rare but important for that decade.

Much more numerous are the papyri in Arabic, all of which naturally date after the Arab conquest of Egypt (639–641). Here it must be said that problems of linguistic competence have all but stymied the integration of different bodies of evidence; indeed, few scholars have worked on the Arabic papyri at all, and thousands lie unread in collections.

John Ray has estimated that more than forty foreign languages were spoken and written in Egypt between the New Kingdom and the Arab conquest.[16] Those mentioned above are obviously only a fraction of this total. It is not an accident that the non-Egyptian languages mentioned are those used for the exercise of their administrative and military power by the foreign powers that conquered Egypt during this period.

WHO WROTE WHAT

Most papyrologists, asked to tell the inquirer what sorts of texts they find on papyri, will make lists. The typology of documentary texts is, more often than not, juridical. Scholars with strong legal interests played an important role in the first decades of papyrology (from the late nineteenth century to the

1920s) and helped to create the typologies which by now have become the common stock. For example, in Orsolina Monte-vecchi's manual of papyrology, as in Eric Turner's book, a series of chapters deals with subdivisions of the documentation, one treating the schools and literary culture, one religion, and one documents. Within Montevecchi's documentary chapter, Latin papyri and "Various aspects of life" get separate sections, and the rest are divided into "Documents sent from private persons to functionaries" and "Acts between private persons." This subdivision omits documentation internal to the administration or emanating from it, which had been treated in an earlier part of the book. Similarly, but with a twist, the typology used in indexing the continuing repertory of documents published outside indexed volumes, the *Sammelbuch*, divides texts into state activity, private law, business affairs, agriculture, cult, and private life. The twist is that these are actually domains of activity, not types of document; classifying leases under private law rather than agriculture, however, suggests that here the document type was primary.

Types of text will be described throughout this book, in a fashion that I hope will make them more meaningful and interesting than their simple enumeration here would be. But there is a more serious and substantive incoherence in lists of this sort, of which a hint has already been given in the remarks above about languages. Many document types occur only in particular languages, or at particular times, or in a given language only at a given period. Even within the Greek papyri distinctions must be drawn. The point may perhaps be illus-trated by considering Montevecchi's category of "Documents sent from private persons to functionaries." Here is the list: (1) census declarations; (2) birth declarations; (3) death de-clarations; (4) epikrisis [status scrutiny] documents; (5) eph-ebic documents; (6) property declarations; (7) requests for the opening of wills; (8) requests for tutors for women and minors; (9) requests for various concessions; (10) petitions; (11) sureties and guarantees. Of these, nos. 1–5 and 7–9 are exclusively of the Roman period,[17] and no. 6 almost exclusively. Thus only the last two categories, petitions and sureties, can have any claim to be typical, represented to some degree in all parts of the millennium from Alexander to the Arabs.

This is not a trivial problem. There is a very pronounced

tendency among papyrologists to view the Roman period – the centuries from Augustus to Diocletian – as normative. In large measure this is simply the result of the much larger quantities of surviving texts from this period, coupled perhaps with the dominant impact on the field of the *Oxyrhynchus Papyri*, in which Ptolemaic texts are virtually absent and those of the post-Diocletianic period less numerous than those of the first three centuries of Roman rule (though numbers for the later centuries are beginning to catch up in the last couple of decades). But the discounting of the 'late' or 'Byzantine' era certainly owes something also to the common disdain for epochs viewed as degenerate,[18] and from a Hellenic point of view the same comparative depreciation has often applied to the Hellenistic world as well. In chapter 3 we will look at the importance of stratifying evidence chronologically, but it is as well to be reminded already that even at the grossest level distinctions among periods are necessary, and no period deserves normative status. The presences and absences of document types have much to teach us about these societies.

So also does a careful consideration of who actually did the writing. It can in general be taken for granted that government officials, other than those who only ran errands, could and did read and write. But this does not mean that those responsible for generating documents were always those who wrote them. At both ends of the spectrum there are exceptions. At the lower end, there were certainly officials who had to sign documents but might get away with only these subscriptions. Such was the now famous Petaüs, village secretary of Ptolemais Hormou in the Arsinoite nome in the reign of Commodus.[19] Petaüs could sign only with difficulty, and sheets showing him practicing his signature survive to testify to the ordeal that doing so caused him (Figure 5). At the other end of the scale, high-ranking officials like *strategoi* of nomes or the prefect of Egypt had secretaries to take down their letters and then copy them into letter-books, even if the official would normally add a greeting to the letter in his own hand.[20] Even the humble village secretaries, in fact, benefited from the availability of professional scribes.

In the private sphere similar phenomena can be observed. A large part of the paperwork generated by wealthier households – internal correspondence, accounts, orders for payment, receipts, and the like – was actually produced not by the owners but by staff, both slave and free. We know that male members of the propertied classes could, with few exceptions, read and write fairly easily; indeed, some were active in literary pursuits. But their means and their volume of activity both permitted and required them to delegate most of the actual writing to others. One might almost say that there was a direct correlation between the social standing that guaranteed literacy and the means to avoid writing. But this should not be taken to mean that men of this standing did not do a fair amount of writing all the same.

Even for those of lesser means, the most critical texts would be written by others. Virtually no legal documents were drafted by private individuals, any more than they are in modern societies. The language needed to be got correct, all the clauses properly worded, if one was not to risk significant economic loss from defects in the agreement. This was the work of professionals. Similarly, if one wished to send a petition to the king, governor, or some other powerful person, one usually employed a skilled professional. These documents are not as stereotyped as contracts, but those of any given period tend to display common tendencies of language and theme, and most are written in rapid, professional hands. Apart from the occasional rough draft, which a well-educated person might undertake to write, then, petitions also cannot be viewed as unmediated representations of the thoughts of those nominally submitting them.

Private letters provide a useful microcosm of the interplay of ability and need to read and write. Some were certainly written by professional scribes, perhaps specializing in letter-writing. Others were obviously and painfully not, composed in the struggling hands characteristic of those whose education never progressed past the most elementary stage. Still others, perhaps the majority, were written in neat, well-formed hands very different from those common among professional scribes but characteristic of those developed by the end of an elementary education. Some of these are certainly autographs of their authors, but it is often difficult to be certain whether we are dealing with the author's handwriting, that of a scribe owned or employed by the author, or even of a public scribe[21] who used this kind of hand as that appropriate for private letters (for greater readability, perhaps). The palaeography of the letters is, in fact, a largely unstudied subject, from which we may eventually hope to learn much more about the day-to-day writing habits of the population.

SURVIVAL OF PAPYRI

No systematic study has ever been made of the paths through which papyri have survived to modern times, been collected by museums and libraries, and been published.[22] What follows is a sketch in broad outline, to which no doubt many exceptions could be cited; but it may at least suggest how the majority of the papyri have come down to us and what sorts of things need to be kept in mind as a result.

For the Ptolemaic period a general distinction may be drawn between those texts derived from cartonnage and those from other sources. Cartonnage is a papier-mâché type product created for the encasement of the mummified bodies both of humans and of animals dedicated to the theriomorphic divinities of Egypt. Scrap paper was bought in bulk by funerary workers, cut as necessary to fit the anatomy of the mummy, layered on and molded around the body, and covered with gesso plaster, on which an image of the deceased was often painted. Some of these mummies have been recovered in controlled excavations, mostly in the late nineteenth and early twentieth centuries, notably those of the British at Hibeh and in the Fayum (especially at Tebtunis), and of the Germans at Abusir el-Melek (in the Nile valley just east of the Fayum). Others have been found in clandestine excavations and sold on the antiquities market, including mainly finds from the Arsinoite, Herakleopolite, and Oxyrhynchite nomes now in a host of European and American collections.

Although the organization of the waste-paper trade in Egypt is unknown to us, it is reasonable to suppose that dealers supplying the funerary industry found it more economical to buy in bulk. The major source for large quantities, of course, was the government, and it is for this reason that the finds of cartonnage are heavily dominated by government files. These are varied in contents and include correspondence, tax documents, officially deposited contracts and wills, legal texts, and other matter. But there are many categories naturally absent from such assemblages, and a picture of Ptolemaic Egypt built up mainly from such sources would greatly overemphasize the role of the state.[23]

Partly balancing this large weight of official texts are the finds of papyri that were not part of cartonnage. These come, almost without exception, from clandestine discoveries and are thus without archaeological context. (They have, however, at least escaped the cutting and pasting that often make cartonnage exceptionally difficult to read.) They include the largest of all papyrological archives, the papers of Zenon, presumed found in the ruins of the village of Philadelphia in the Arsinoite nome, but also other very large groups such as the archives of various military families from Pathyris, the archive of the Memphite Sarapieion, the papers of the Theban funerary workers, and several somewhat smaller groups. On the whole, Demotic texts play a large role in all of the Upper Egyptian archives of this type, and it is probable that most if not all of these groups were found stored in jars or boxes, either in houses in dry areas or in tombs. This mass of material often involves the official activities of the persons who collected the papers, but there is a far higher proportion of documentation of private economic affairs, particularly contracts and, especially in the Zenon archive, private letters.

It is evident, however, that these two groups, even taken together, represent only a few of the possible motives for creating and saving papers, mainly the interests of government operations and of private property transactions. Most importantly, we have virtually no finds from Ptolemaic habitation sites. More than ordinary caution is therefore needed in dealing with silences in the documentary record from this period.

With the Roman period things change dramatically. After the Augustan period cartonnage plays virtually no role, and finds from habitation sites grow enormously. The British and, subsequently, Italian excavations at Oxyrhynchos produced tens of thousands of papyri, and despite the large number still unpublished the quantity of material edited to date is large enough to make of Oxyrhynchos something of a papyrological standard. Other scientific excavations have also been productive, including those at Karanis and, for ostraka, the recent excavations at Mons Claudianus in the eastern desert. The Oxyrhynchos papyri came mainly from ancient rubbish dumps, but in the case of Mons Claudianus, Karanis, Elkab, and now

Kellis, at least part of the finds come from houses and other buildings, information about which has been carefully recorded to allow correlation of papyrological and archaeological data.[24] Enormous quantities of Greek texts of the Roman period have also come from uncontrolled, unofficial excavations of city and village sites, and most European and American papyrus collections derive mainly from purchases on the antiquities market. In these cases little, if any, contextual information is usually available, and the task of reconstructing archival masses is made difficult by the common dispersion of groups among several collections. As a result, new bits of known archives keep turning up.

For the Roman period we have a much wider range of documents than for the Ptolemaic, and it is a natural question how far this is a result of the stark differences in the ways in which papyri have reached us from the two periods, how far an actual reflection of changes in government, law, economy, and society. This, again, is a question to which no serious study has ever been given.

The pattern of discoveries in the Roman period is essentially continued for the late Roman and Byzantine periods, but even less of the material comes from controlled excavations, with Oxyrhynchos continuing as a prime source. A major difference, however, is that much of the Roman material comes from villages, especially from the Arsinoite, whereas the post-fourth-century papyri come almost entirely from cities (Arsinoe, Antinoopolis, Hermopolis, Oxyrhynchos), with the single exception of Aphrodito, which was anything but a typical village. There is thus a considerable change in the texture of the documentation, and once again serious questions arise about the comparability of the finds for the two periods.

There are other factors that complicate the picture given thus far. Probably the most salient is the almost total lack of material surviving from the Delta, where the desert conditions favorable to survival of papyrus do not obtain. So far only two routes to the preservation of material from this large region have been found. One is for texts written in the Delta to have been taken elsewhere in Egypt and to have survived there. For example, nome *strategoi* in the Roman period routinely served outside their home district, and when they stepped down and returned home, they took some of their papers with them. This is, for

example, probably the explanation for the survival of the roll
of census declarations from the Prosopite nome.[25] There are no
doubt many such papyri that we cannot identify as such. The
other is for fire to have carbonized the papyrus rolls, leaving
them less vulnerable to later destruction – although immensely
difficult to unroll, preserve, and read. Two such masses have
appeared so far, one from Thmuis and one from Boubastos; in
both cases publication is underway but much work remains.[26]
In all of these cases the texts have been extremely instructive,
reflecting in form, style, and contents a high degree of commonality with finds elsewhere in Egypt, but preserving significant information about the Delta that could not have been
obtained otherwise. They thus form an important means of
measuring the gravity of the loss to historical study suffered as
a result of the geographical lopsidedness of the surviving finds.

For the areas to the east and west of the Nile valley, on the
other hand, a similar silence prevailed until the last couple of
decades. But finds of ostraka in the eastern desert and the oases
of the western desert, excavations at coastal sites on the Red
Sea, and excavations in the western oases have brought thousands of texts to light in recent years.[27] As these are published,
the distinctive societies, economies, and ecologies of these
regions are starting to come into focus.

There is no single or simple lesson to be drawn from the
pattern of discoveries, but it must always be kept in mind that
for any given period a high proportion of the total known
documents comes from a fairly small number of discoveries.
Once again, this fact will have little impact on some questions,
where randomness is not important to representativeness, but
in other matters, drawing generalizable conclusions may be
seriously compromised.

RESTORING AND USING DAMAGED PAPYRI

The preceding sections have been about ways in which our
documentation with papyri is fragmentary, in two senses: only
some types of activity were ever documented at all, and much
of what was has not survived. Even what does survive, however,
is also often fragmentary, and something needs to be said about
the use of fragmentary texts.[28]
Editors generally present restored texts, in which they supply

as much of the missing text as they can; by convention, such text is enclosed inside square brackets: [lost letters]. Such restorations in general depend on a two-part analysis, although the process may be so rapid at times – especially with a lightly damaged papyrus and an experienced editor – that the editor is not conscious of the stages. The first stage is the analysis of what survives. Often, it is immediately clear, if the damage is not too great or diagnostic phrases survive, what kind of text we are dealing with. If it is not so clear, a rigorous analysis of the vocabulary or other formal characteristics of the surviving part will often allow the editor to discover what it is. The second stage comes in finding parallels, examining texts of the same kind. These two aspects are, naturally, iterative rather than entirely sequential.

Very straightforward, formulaic texts often yield in their entirety to this approach; tax receipts are perhaps the most straightforward example. In other instances, standardization of elements is relatively high, but there is considerable variation in their order, extent of abbreviations, and precise phrasing, particularly from place to place and time to time. This is the case with land leases. Here a more exacting analysis of the remains is necessary in order to establish the syntax and flow of thought through the document. Such a restoration may be somewhat less complete than that of a tax receipt, but as in absolutely standard texts the major problems lie in such contingent information as names and numbers.

As documents become less standard, the task becomes harder. In petitions, for example, similar stories are told somewhat differently from case to case, even from draft to draft of the same petition. Here the editor's task moves increasingly away from the mechanical use of parallels and into the attempt to understand the text on its own terms, borrowing phrases where appropriate, seeking to figure out what parts of a construction are missing, and in effect trying to become a member of the writer's time and culture.

At the extreme end of the scale, documents that are not at all standard often cannot be restored at all once their damage exceeds narrow limits – cannot be restored, that is, with any confidence that one is actually reproducing the original language or even thought. Editors and critics often succumb to the temptation to rewrite the lost text, but that must be viewed as an exercise in prose composition, not as restoration, and the historian uses such reinvented texts at his or her peril.

A still larger problem must be kept in mind by the user of papyrus texts: restorations represent to a large extent an exercise in circularity. Editors can restore with confidence in a document only what they already know, either from the remains on the papyrus, or from parallels. The act of restoration does not usually add to the store of knowledge;[29] it is the arguments underpinning a restoration that bring new knowledge. What cannot be restored, conversely, is precisely what was unique – the number of artabas of wheat to be paid in rent each year, the names of the parties to an agreement, the identity of a person complained against, and so on.

The significance of this logical difficulty lies in the use made of texts by subsequent readers. Anything put on the page as a restoration is almost certain to wind up being used by some later scholar or, just as bad, the presence of restoration will lead to the entire text's being discounted. Considerable caution is therefore required of the editor, and the "purely illustrative" or "exempli gratia" restorations beloved of editors belong in the notes, where they can be read for what they are, not in the text. Often enough, texts are reprinted, whether in the original or in translation, in subsequent collections, usually stripped of the accompanying notes where cautions are raised or the reliability of restorations carefully assessed.

From this perspective, restorations are mainly a device for presenting an analysis and interpretation of a text in a readily usable fashion; a continuous text is, after all, far more readable than a block of discontinuous words and a mass of notes. A translation of such a restored text is similarly a device of presentation, a means of clarifying an interpretation. But the historian who would use such texts must always keep in mind that restorations are a form of presentation of an argument, not simply another form of primary evidence messed up with some funny brackets.

Chapter 3

Particular and general

It will be evident from the varied circumstances in which papyri have survived and been edited that they reach the scholar and student with a great diversity of immediate contexts. At one extreme, a papyrus may be acquired in isolation through the antiquities market, with no associated information about where it was found or with what other texts. At the other, a papyrus may be found as part of a group in a controlled excavation or at least be identifiable as a member of an assemblage of papyri. (Papyrologists often refer to such assemblages loosely as "archives," not necessarily meaning to ascribe to them either an official capacity or even any ancient physical unity.[1])

The task of the historian in using papyri is clearly conditioned to a large extent by these circumstances. In an extreme case the author and recipient of a text may be unknown, and the conditions under which it was drawn up a matter of conjecture. Or all of the persons may be well known, along with their family connections, material circumstances, and the context of writing. These differing cases impose different tasks on the historian. The purpose of this chapter is to show several instances of the scholar's response to the challenge offered by a papyrus or group of papyri. In the first section we will look at two papyri lacking an obvious context, from which historians have managed to extract a great deal; the first of these is in fact close to the first of the extremes described above. With them I discuss a text forming part of an archive but the subject of important study from a viewpoint outside that archive and a foray into massive tax rolls for a purpose very different from the usual. A second section will consider various ways in which clusters or assemblages of documents allow rich and informative analysis.

The third section will speak briefly – because the question will occupy us again in various forms in later chapters – of the process of synthesizing scattered bits of information; in the fourth we will look at the ways in which absent papyrological information can be replaced by other types of evidence.

UNDERSTANDING INDIVIDUAL DOCUMENTS

One of the richest and most influential studies of bilingualism in Ptolemaic Egypt was published twenty years ago by Roger Rémondon. It is founded on a single papyrus text, and a small one at that, just nine short lines written on part of a tall, thin strip of material.[2] In its entirety, the text reads as follows:

> Finding out that you are learning Egyptian letters, I rejoice for you and for myself, because now when you return to the city you will teach boys at the house of the enema-doctor Phalou..es, and you will have a means of support for old age.

A single sentence, written as if part of a letter but devoid of greeting or conclusion. Date (probably second century BC) and provenance are unknown. The precise nature of the text is doubtful; it might be an extract, or a draft, and the presence of washed-out text on the other side of the papyrus only makes matters more obscure.

Not a very promising situation, one might say, but all the more an opportunity for a virtuoso performance. The point of departure is the fact that the author was a woman (the opening participle is feminine). Previous editors had supposed this was a mother writing to her young son, but Rémondon argues that the recipient cannot be a child or youth, on the grounds that (1) the language suggests a degree of distance – both physical and emotional – between the two parties, which is "scarcely compatible with the relations of son to mother"; (2) the recipient is already old enough to become a teacher on his return to the city, hence adult; (3) a Greek could not have learned Egyptian as a child, but only after having completed his Greek education; (4) a Greek would thus have had to be an adult to learn written Egyptian. From this he concludes further that the author is the recipient's wife, not his mother.

The core of Rémondon's discussion is an investigation of what this man was going to be teaching, and to whom; all of

those who had written about the text had supposed that this
would be Greek, and the audience had been taken by most to
be the children of Phalou..es. Rémondon's argument first
rejects the latter notion; unless Phalou..es had young children
and produced a virtually endless supply of them, the notion that
this teaching would provide support for the recipient's old age
makes no sense. He then proceeds to argue convincingly that
the carefully worded Greek cannot in any case mean this; the
"boys" (*paidaria*) are not those *of* Phalou..es, but *at* Phalou..es'
establishment. This leads Rémondon to see the establishment
as a school, specifically one based on Phalou..es' medical
specialty, healing by the administration of enemas, a typically
Egyptian medical practice. The *paidaria*, he argues, were more
likely young slaves than free apprentices. The training of slaves
as doctors to enhance their value is otherwise known and
indeed fairly common. Rémondon cites evidence for the popularity of Egyptian medical practices among the Greeks and
Romans to show that there would have been a market for the
products of the kind of school he is supposing.

We return then to the question of what this man would be
teaching. Rémondon points out that the evidence for slavery in
Ptolemaic Egypt shows that slaves were overwhelmingly not
Egyptians but imported, and though in many cases not originally Greek, at least Greek-speaking. A school run by an Egyptian
doctor, teaching an Egyptian medical specialty (like most such
lore thought to be teachable only in its own language) to Greek-
speaking slaves, and needing a language teacher: surely this
must be a teacher of Egyptian. This is in any case the natural
reading of a sequence of thought that runs "you have learned
Egyptian; therefore you can teach."

The argument thus far is based on three main pillars: close
analysis of the language, information from other sources about
the cultural context, and "common-sense" rejection of some
possibilities on the basis of underlying assumptions about
human behavior. It is thus a good example of traditional
philological method, seeking above all to explain the text,
expertly applied. The arguments are vulnerable to attack from
different or developed notions of the cultural context and, still
more immediately, from different notions of human behavior.
Most notably, perhaps, the assumption that there could not be
estrangement between mother and teenage son – but could

readily be between husband and wife – may seem to us to be a product of a specific modern social and chronological context and at least open to question. That particular point, however, can be discarded without grave damage to the overall flow of reasoning. This is not the end of the article. Rémondon proceeds to try to disengage some broader implications for the Hellenistic society of Egypt. Claiming that our man was serving the slaves' masters directly, rather than becoming an employee of Phalou..es, he rejects any notion that this papyrus is testimony to a greater complexity in the relations of Greek and Egyptians than was found a century earlier, much less that economic class was overtaking ethnicity as the main determinant of status (as Rostovtzeff had supposed). What Rémondon sees, instead, is a cultural phenomenon that he describes as "an absolutely negative experience." He sees the main element pushing Greeks to learn Egyptian as a desire to gain access to specifically Egyptian knowledge in medicine, religion, and other areas. But this access appears to him to have been kept in tight compartments precisely because the Greeks sought to maintain their vision of Egypt as a static, controlled curiosity rather than as a living, autonomous society, one with which it might really be necessary to come to terms culturally.

This further development of the argument is clearly of a different kind from what precedes. Instead of depending on the close analysis of the document itself, it is based on some broad arguments about cultural trends, which the papyrus is then held to exemplify. The result is certainly a considerable increase in the interest and richness of the text itself, but a decline in the rigor of the analysis. Perhaps more to the point, the nature of the study passes from the use of the text to illuminate Ptolemaic Egypt to the reverse. These stages of an argument, of course, are not always so clearly distinguishable, and they may be more recursive than in this article.

This is, to be sure, chosen as an extreme case of a complex argument developed from an exceptionally small amount of text, for which the entire context must be derived from argument and analogy, but where even the most obtuse observer could see at a glance that fundamental historical issues were at stake. Quite the reverse is often true, as in the case of routine texts, particularly lists. An example is *P.Amst.* I 72, a list of names, again with no provenance or explicit date, broken on two sides and full of apparently commonplace names. The editors, noting that one person in the list was a city councillor (*bouleutes*), assigned a date after AD 202 because the cities of Egypt lacked city councils before they were granted them by Septimius Severus. They also pointed out that none of the individuals listed was given the Latin family name Aurelius, which was distributed *en masse* to the population through Caracalla's grant of citizenship in the Antonine Constitution, and from this they suggested that the papyrus must date before 212.[3] The editors did not offer any overall interpretation of the purpose of the longer list from which this fragment came, but they pointed out that most, if not all, of the persons listed were indicated to have gone by a different name at an earlier time.

This apparently uninteresting list might have remained buried under its banality had not Peter van Minnen turned an attentive eye to the names in the list.[4] He noticed first that linguistic elements in some of the names, and several of the names themselves, pointed to an origin in the Delta. Many Egyptian names are characteristic of particular regions, even of fairly restricted localities, and such assignments of provenance on the basis of onomastic evidence are not uncommon. The comparative evidence for the Delta is too sparse to allow one to be certain what part of it was the source of the papyrus, but the attribution to the region appears sufficiently secure.

More importantly, however, van Minnen recognized that some of the new names assumed by persons in the list were translations into Greek of their former names, which had uniformly been Egyptian names in Greek transliteration. Thus Pibichis, "the one of the falcon," becomes Hierax, the Greek word for the same bird. Not all of the names can be explained in this fashion, but at least 70 percent can, and perhaps more; our knowledge of Egyptian names is still very imperfect. As van Minnen notes, similar translations of Egyptian names into Greek occur elsewhere; what is noteworthy about the Amsterdam papyrus is the regularity and concentration of cases in a particular population, presumably part of the citizen body of a nome capital in the Delta. He asks if the introduction of city councils after 202 led to large-scale changes in nomenclature, especially among the relatively wealthy part of the population that took up membership in the new councils.[5] Such a change would be an aspect of the process whereby the bilingual upper classes of the cities became fully absorbed during the course of the third century into political and social structures common to Greek cities throughout the Roman East, and thus a matter of considerable historical interest.[6]

The recognition of the pattern of name-changes, like noticing the geographical affinity of the names, is in itself principally a matter of an attentive application of philological method, in this case, however, including linguistic analysis of the Egyptian elements of the names. The point at which van Minnen's argument passes on to broader implications, however, again depends on a particular understanding of the context of political life in the early third century.

One important underpinning is the editors' dating to 202–212, which van Minnen does not question. The *terminus post quem* is secure enough, but the *terminus ante quem* is not, because official lists of this period do not generally include the *nomen* before individuals' Greek names.[7] The absence of Aurelius is therefore probably without significance. If, however, this date is insecure, there may be consequences for the interpretation of the list. Both editors and van Minnen suppose (the latter explicitly) that the point of listing previous names in the list was that the changes were relatively recent; though not demonstrable, this point is reasonable enough. If the papyrus were dated to *c.* 225 rather than to 202–212, the identification of the institution of the councils as the trigger for the onomastic change might no longer be easily defensible. In that case, the specific link of Severus' reform to the adoption of Hellenic names by Egyptians would collapse.

Methodologically, the central point is that van Minnen reasonably presents his idea as a hypothesis, rather than as a firmly established conclusion. It should be possible both in reviewing other published texts and in editing new ones to be alert to evidence – more precisely dated, one would hope – that would either show that a later date is likely (and hence a new hypothesis desirable) or that the phenomenon already existed in the first decade of the century, in which case the hypothesis would still have a fair chance of being sound.

The third individual document is part of the large and well-known sixth-century archive of Dioskoros, which will turn up in other contexts (including the next section of this chapter). It is a banker's loan taken out in Constantinople in 541 by two emissaries of their home village of Aphrodito, in Upper Egypt, who were in the capital representing its interests.[8] (One of them was Dioskoros' father Apollos.) It has often been studied and cited in connection with the affairs of the village and its long struggle to maintain its autonomy in tax collection. A recent article of James Keenan, however, reverses the perspective, asking what this amounts to as a banking transaction.[9] Instead of attempting an analysis of the kinds discussed above, Keenan provides a narrative of the transaction, trying to look at it both from the point of view of the borrowers – why did they borrow, how could they have paid it back – and of the lender – who was he, and how did these people fit into his banking activity. Much of what emerges is unanswerable questions, like how the banker would have proceeded in case of a default, given that the security for the loan was located in Egypt, far from the banker's base of operations.

The use of narrative here is, as Keenan notes, the exception rather than the rule in papyrological history-writing, however much narrative may be the form of history most commonly assumed by philosophers of history. Keenan remarks, "The links in the stories that are founded on such facts are sometimes speculative and imaginative, calculated guesses that are not clinically verifiable." But he believes that they retain "the explanatory function, the cognitive instrumentality that the practice of history demands." Only a relatively small handful of papyri offer the raw material for such an approach to be more than trivially useful, but where it can be used (in addition to, not in place of, other approaches), it has the ability to force on the historian a set of questions about just how the events in question actually could have occurred. These questions may be answerable or not – there are some of each in this case – but in either event they lead forward our understanding of the situation.

Such intensive scrutiny of individual texts has obvious affinities to what has been called "microhistory," although it does not necessarily invoke the ideological underpinnings sometimes present in microhistory.[10] What is sought is not necessarily the typical but the individual, making choices and acting within the constraints of the possible. Peter Parsons, in discussing private letters, has remarked, "The easier explanation may be right: ordinary people thought in cliches. Even so, one does seem to hear, from time to time, an individual voice." Parsons proceeds to identify a number of such individual voices, making no claim for them except that they stand out from the ordinary.[11]

Perhaps the most interesting instance of the identification of an individual voice is Herbert Youtie's celebrated paper at the Ann Arbor Congress of Papyrology in 1968, which provides an exceptional insight into the possibilities of literary culture and its uses in the Egyptian villages.[12] In studying the tax rolls from Karanis, Youtie describes a formal characteristic of the rolls: that in many entries the scribe had indicated that the taxes were actually paid by an agent or lessee of the person who was liable for them. Such indications were given by putting the name of the actual payer in parentheses after that of the legal taxpayer. He noticed, moreover, that whereas the legal taxpayer's name was recorded with great formality and regularity, the physical payer's name might be recorded in varying ways in different entries. But something more caught his attention: some of the names inside parentheses, although Greek words, were not known Greek names. Rather, they were literal Greek renderings of the Egyptian names by which people were known.

The final example Youtie offered concerned a Greek word referring to the tongue of a mousetrap, used to render an Egyptian name meaning "mousecatcher" or "mousetrap." This word is found, in extant Greek, only in a fragment of Callimachus. Youtie (1970: 550–1) points out that this, like his other examples,

> is a possible translation for the Egyptian name to which it corresponds, but it is not itself in the tradition of Greek names. And none of these words would be helpful in identifying the person whom it designates. The poetic and rare ἀνδίκτης would have no existence for most Greeks of average education. They certainly never heard the word spoken, and almost certainly never saw it written. Not many Greeks or Graeco-Egyptians at Karanis were in the habit of entertaining themselves with Callimachus. . . . For us, however, these "names" resurrect an anonymous but well delineated

personality. Among the clerks in the tax bureau was one whose role as *érudit manqué* comes through to us even after so long a time. The linguistic facility, the literary culture once so promising and now so pointless, the trivial display for no eyes but his own, the light and barely sarcastic touch – they are all there. And what could be more satisfying to a tax clerk with pretensions to learning than a borrowing from Callimachus furtively inserted into a gigantic money register, where no one would ever notice it?'

ARCHIVES AND DOSSIERS

Much of the most productive historical study of Egypt has come from the study of "archives" (in the broad sense of that term), collections of papers around an individual, a family, or an office.[13] With isolated documents, a substantial part of the interpreter's effort generally goes into providing as far as possible an immediate context. As we have seen, extending beyond that to broader significance usually involves a substantial leap into a more speculative mode, often with no way to test the hypotheses involved. Where an archive exists, by contrast, it is often possible to establish the immediate context with a fairly high degree of confidence and through straightforward methods. The attempt to set out the broader significance then rests on a more solid footing and more readily escapes circularity.

In many cases the starting point of investigation is the firm establishment of the identity and interests of an individual. A good example is the first-century (AD) tax archive from Philadelphia, centered on the figure of Nemesion son of Zoilos, which is scattered among many collections and in the process of comprehensive editing by Ann Hanson. Reconstructing the archive is itself an iterative process, in which clues allow the historian to delineate enough of an individual's characteristics to permit attribution of further documents to the archive; these in turn deepen the complexity of the portrait of the individual and his milieu and allow the process to continue.[14] Until the full archive is published, in fact, it is only the editor with access to the unedited texts and to corrected texts of the previously edited papyri who can see the person and setting fully.

The collection and analysis of Nemesion's papers allow some

characteristics of his position in society, his outlook, and his behavior to become clear. For instance, Nemesion's papers include the draft of a petition, probably to the prefect of Egypt, asking him to order the centurion in the area of Philadelphia to compel Nemesion's colleague in a tax-collecting position to attend to his duties.[15] The first editor of this papyrus, unable to read Nemesion's name in full and not recognizing his handwriting, concentrated his commentary on various questions of taxes, administration, and law. Hanson was able not only to place the draft in the archive, but to show from several other examples that Nemesion was in the habit of invoking the aid of high Roman officials in support of his work as a tax collector. An isolated case thus becomes part of a pattern of behavior.

That behavior can in turn be linked to other aspects of Nemesion's activity, including his business interests (farming, sheep raising, moneylending), his cozy relationships with other wealthy and powerful residents of his village, his access to the use of armed men to enforce his will, his possession of a copy of Claudius' letter to the Alexandrians, and his use of a couple of Roman calendrical habits. Nemesion, in short, was a characteristic example of the local elites of the Roman provinces, offered opportunities for power and wealth by the imperial rulers in return for supporting, identifying with, and enforcing Roman rule in their own localities. Although his home was a village in rural Egypt, not a Greek city of coastal Asia Minor, the pattern is one familiar to us from the epigraphical as well as the papyrological documentation. The reconstitution of the archive has thus provided enough information about an individual and his milieu to allow clear definition of his characteristics on a secure basis. Their typicality, their lack of surprises, in turn allow the broader context to confirm that the reconstruction of the particular is reasonable.

Dossiers need not be large or provide typical figures to be useful and diagnostic. A remarkable example is provided by a cluster of documents within the sixth-century Aphrodito papyri. Although this assemblage largely deals with the notary, landowner, and poet Dioskoros and the affairs of his family, it is not exclusively concerned with them. James Keenan has identified a subdossier in these papers concerned with the affairs of Aurelius Phoibammon, son of Triadelphos, whom he describes as a "land entrepreneur."[16] Phoibammon figures in a striking group of three papyri which document his transactions with a soldier named Flavius Samuel, who owned a farm of 28 arouras in Aphrodito but was himself stationed elsewhere. In 526 Samuel leased this farm to Phoibammon at a good rent (140 artabas of wheat and barley per year), but at the same time borrowed from him – in effect, received as advance rent – a combination of money and grain worth substantially more than the entire first year's rent. In lieu of interest, Phoibammon received a reduction in the rent of about 11 percent, meaning that the rent payable was only a little more than half the value of the loan.

This may not have been the parties' first transaction, and it certainly was not their last. About a year later, Samuel borrowed another 30 artabas of grain from Phoibammon; and another month or two after that, Samuel borrowed another 18 artabas and gave Phoibammon a mortgage on the farm. It is hardly surprising that the editor of the first and third texts, published in 1955,[17] wondered if Samuel ever managed to extricate himself from Phoibammon, or that the editor of the middle agreement, published in 1977, concludes that Samuel surely lost the farm. Samuel's consumption needs certainly appear to have been such as to make him unable to let the remaining income start to pay down the principal of the loans.

The later editor comments, "These three papyri show how a small farmer gradually lost his property to a rich landowner" (*P.Mich.* XIII, p. 106). That, of course, is what one would expect; it is the recurring story told about rich and poor landowners throughout antiquity, a staple of class struggle going back at least as far as Solon. But in this case it is wrong. It is wrong partly because Flavius Samuel was not the small farmer of the morality play. He was a soldier, a relatively privileged person (with "Flavius" as a mark of his rank), and the absentee owner of a good-sized farm, perhaps two to three times what was needed to support an average family. And it is wrong partly (and more importantly) because Keenan's examination of the little dossier of Phoibammon – a dozen texts beyond this trio – shows that he is far from the stereotyped rich landowner. It is the latter point that interests us here.

Most of Phoibammon's dossier documents lease transactions, in which he was the lessee for owners who could not or would not farm their lands themselves. Five of these were institutions, two absentee landowners, and two local owners, one woman and one man who probably owned more than he could farm personally. Phoibammon certainly owned some land himself, but the documented activity concerns mainly his filling a particular niche in the economy, the entrepreneur who saves the owner the trouble of being a farmer, assuring him, her, or it a fixed income and assuming significant risk in return for the possibility of substantial profit. Both the Samuel papers and some of the others suggest that Phoibammon had accumulated enough reserves in grain to be able to pay rent in advance when it was useful. He also acquired various parcels of land over his long (at least 46 years) career.

The overall picture that emerges from this small group of texts, then, is of a figure absent from the traditional rural mythology: the entrepreneur, of middling means, owning some land himself, leasing land from others, sometimes subleasing what he took from others, lending money and produce – sometimes in return for leverage or the chance of foreclosing, and through wit and industry accumulating capital that he can invest in further such transactions. If Phoibammon were unique in these characteristics, Keenan's delineation of his activity might make us uneasy, but the pattern is in fact documented also in some other village archives, most notably, perhaps, the archive of Aurelius Isidoros, from the fourth century. The comparatively small number of documents involved gives the conclusions reached here less certainty than, say, in the case of Nemesion, and Keenan acknowledges that some of his re-construction has speculative elements. But it raises important questions about how far one can generalize from the evidence from a particular place and what patterns may have been typical.

Not all archives center on individuals or families. A striking case in which we possess part of a true official archive is the group of registers of contracts from the village of Tebtunis dating to the reign of Claudius, which belonged originally to the village record office, or *grapheion*.[18] These list the essential information about each contract registered during the time period covered by the register: type of contract, parties, object, and amounts of money. They thus give a comprehensive view of the transactions in a particular village during a particular year (or part of a year) that the parties (or more specifically, the party to whom obligations were created) thought it worthwhile to record in writing and to register. Such a body of material, evidently, offers many opportunities for analysis.

One such approach to this archive is a study by Deborah Hobson of the role of women in the economic life of the village.[19] She begins with a simple enumeration of the transactions in which women appear. More than half of these have to do with the documentation of women's marital property rights (settlements at marriage, receipts of dowry, return of dowry). There are three wet-nursing contracts, and a scattering of sales and leases concerning real property (usually houses) and slaves. Rare or absent are sales of land, sales of animals, service contracts, and leases of land. Hobson (1984a: 380) concludes that women "do not seem to participate in the agricultural or commercial life of the village directly" and that their appearances mostly have to do with the regulation of their roles as wives and daughters in the system of transmission of property.

Such conclusions are obviously interesting in their own right, and because of the village-wide scope one can easily avoid the traps involved in working with a single, possibly atypical, family.[20] On the other hand, the brevity of the summaries and absence of detail about the families involved makes it impossible to reach any depth in the understanding of the circumstances behind these transactions. More importantly, perhaps, the register gives us a photograph of a particular village at a particular moment. Can one get beyond those limits?

For once we are lucky. Portions of registers have survived for three different years, and the latter two are known to be a period of economic distress caused by a poor (in this case, excessive) Nile flood. The overall pattern of women's independent transactions under these circumstances is not drastically different, but they appear far more often than before in relation to male members of their families. Contracts showing net addition of assets (alimentary contracts, dowries) decline sharply, while those showing net withdrawal of assets (return of dowry) rise. Hobson suggests that men had to use such assets as working capital in times when they were hard pressed and their own assets proved inadequate. Wet-nursing contracts, another means for a woman to provide her husband with capital, also rise. Women appear, moreover, as parties to loans (mostly as co-borrowers with male relatives) more frequently than before. On the whole, then, women still "are on the whole not really economic agents in their own right" (Hobson 1984a: 386). Their role is mainly, even if not exclusively, as holders of assets received through the relatively egalitarian inheritance system of the Egyptian population. These are in a sense the reserve assets, and "the inclusion of women in their capacity as wives is almost an index of the economic plight of the village: the more often they appear linked to their spouses in joint liability, the higher seems to be the general level of debt" (Hobson 1984a: 389). The availability of the data for the bad harvest years thus allows considerable deepening of the conclusions reached from a more normal year, not contradicting what is found there but helping to explain how that pattern was in turn part of a larger picture.

There is no obvious reason why what emerges from this examination of Tebtunis should not be more broadly true, but it is still desirable to test these conclusions as far as they can be. This is in fact possible for the thesis that women's economic role is mainly limited to their households and the assets connected with them; another study by Hobson, this time of the large body of material from Roman Soknopaiou Nesos (a village in another part of the Arsinoite), had already led her to similar conclusions.[21]

The studies based on archives described so far are embodied in articles of moderate length, in part because the bodies of material are not large (as in the case of Phoibammon), in part because the studies focus on particular aspects of larger dossiers. In a number of cases, however, the larger archives have given birth to book-length synthetic studies, attempting to reconstruct particular societies in greater detail.[22] One recent example will be discussed here in some detail. It is a study of the Heroninos archive by Dominic Rathbone (1991).[23] This archive includes some 450 published papyri (Rathbone estimates that another 600 remain unpublished) from a trove found around the beginning of the twentieth century at Theadelphia, another Arsinoite village. It concerns one portion of the estates of Aurelius Appianus, a wealthy and high-ranking Alexandrian.

Heroninos managed the Theadelphian unit of Appianus' holdings during the middle of the third century AD, and the archive consists largely of accounts and letters, now dispersed among various European collections.

Rathbone aims, apart from providing a guide to the Heroninos archive, to set out what he believes are the implications of the published texts for our understanding of the economic character of the estates described in this documentation and, more ambitiously, for land management in the Roman world. He argues that this evidence helps to fill three key gaps in our knowledge left by the literary and archaeological evidence for Roman estates: (1) labor systems outside Italy; (2) method and aims of management; and (3) social and economic relationships of the various people involved. The conclusions, broadly speaking, are the following: These estates were owned by provincial magnates, some of whom were Alexandrian notables and others of whom had equestrian procuratorial careers. Their estates in the Arsinoite nome were directed by members of the local elite, particularly city councillors of Arsinoe who surely had substantial landholdings of their own. The estates also had links to every other level of rural society; the managers (*phrontistai*) of the individual estate units (*phrontides*) came from prosperous rural families.

The labor force of the estates was entirely free, with no trace of slave labor.[24] A core workforce was employed regularly, some of them permanently. Other persons were hired on a more casual basis as needed, and some tasks were contracted out to entirely independent parties. Practices varied considerably from one *phrontis* to another, depending on the type of land, the crops produced, and the style of operation resulting from these constraints. Except for the permanent employees, most workers belonged to the middle and lower strata of rural society. Their work for the estate furnished only a portion of family income, which came otherwise from a very diversified set of sources.

The estate as a whole, with its multiple holdings, aimed at much more than supplying most of its own wants via internal transfers of produce. Rather, it was fundamentally oriented toward production of surpluses of marketable products. In the case of the *phrontis* at Theadelphia (from which this archive comes), that meant above all wine. This goal fits with other evidence for economic rationalism: a centrally managed transport system, close central supervision of inputs and production, and above all a sophisticated accounting system in which all costs were recorded in structured syntheses expressed in cash (whether incurred in reality on credit, in kind, or by actual cash payments), and in which there was a constant concern to control costs of production. An analytic purpose for accounts is suggested also by the abstract use of *ergatai* to mean "mandays of labor" and *zeuge* to mean "days of labor by a team of oxen." Central overhead costs are distributed to the units. The estate appears as an essentially economic enterprise, not an enclosed mini-society run for largely non-economic purposes.

How far this picture can be extrapolated, either back in time in Egypt or across the rest of the Roman empire, is of course still more interesting. Rathbone argues that the second-century accounts from the archive of "the descendants of Laches" (also from the Fayum[25]) prefigure the rational accounting of the Heroninos archive, and that one must at least not assume that the Egyptian situation is unique. He notes that most accounts on papyrus have no context; their potential function in a system of accounts is thus impossible to determine. Only occasionally can an entire system of accounts be seen whole. Here, then, the survival of the accounts as part of a very large archive provides a most unusual opportunity to provide larger meaning to what normally is opaque.

The archive has, however, its silences. We lack all but the scantiest of documentation from the central Arsinoite headquarters of the estate, to say nothing of whatever central management Appianus and his staff exercised in Alexandria. Two of Rathbone's most central theses depend on inference about what management in Arsinoe did. First, they are supposed to have received the balance of estate wine production after expenses were met, somewhere between a fifth and a third of the total, and then marketed it for cash. Second, they are inferred to have taken the monthly summary accounts from the individual *phrontides* and analyzed them for cost efficiency. There are good arguments for both of these positions, which are central to the hypothesis of economic rationality as Rathbone offers it. But because the surviving documentation comes from Theadelphia, not Arsinoe, we see central management only in its relationship to the unit, not in its own activities.

Rathbone's depiction of the Heroninos archive could take on

added interest from comparison with the Zenon archive (the largest of the Ptolemaic period, just as Heroninos is the largest of the Roman), although Rathbone engages in no such comparison. Seventy years ago, Rostovtzeff[26] depicted the activities of Zenon, the energetic manager of the large landholding in the Arsinoite nome of an important resident of Alexandria (in this case the *dioiketes* Apollonios), 500 years before the Heroninos archive, in terms strikingly similar to those Rathbone uses. Apollonios' estate was run, Rostovtzeff argued, with entrepreneurial rationality, a zeal for economic growth, and a strong interest in new crops and new methods. Although Rathbone's Heroninos innovates mainly in details of account-keeping and his Appianus is interested in stability more than in growth, the parallel is nonetheless remarkable. To some critics, of course, the parallel might mean only that two scholars, studying different archives, had been led by a priori assumptions to impose similar views on the material they studied; the ancients are generally thought to have been much less innovative in such matters. But despite some possible overstatement of matters in both instances, this seems to me an unjustified view.

In the case of the Heroninos archive, two very important methodological gains result from the study of the material as an ensemble. First, letters and accounts, the main constituents of this archive, are precisely the two types of text preserved in large quantities that generally frustrate their readers the most, because not just some but almost all of their significance derives from knowing their context, from knowing what their writers knew but we do not. The ability to connect them to one another in quantity is what makes the analysis of this archive work for Rathbone, and it must not be forgotten that underlying the historical superstructure here is an enormous amount of painstaking analysis in detail. Second, the archive so analyzed is rich enough to support the application and testing of a reasonably complex model of economic behavior derived from larger debates on the nature of the ancient economy. It is most unusual that any single archive can contribute directly to such debates in ancient history. The use of models from the social sciences will be discussed further in later chapters.

SYNTHESIZING DISPERSED TEXTS

Often enough, in the absence of major archives, the historian's task is to pick up scattered clues in different documents and link them up, whether in a suggestive pattern or in a tight interlock. A particularly rich instance of this process is provided by an article of Willy Clarysse with the deceptively unassuming title "Some Greeks in Egypt."[27] This article treats three cases of Greeks integrated into Egyptian society. The first is a Greek man, Monimos son of Kleandros, who appears in a Demotic census list of the late third century BC with his wife Esoueris, daughter Demetria, and slave girl Sostrate. By itself this appearance has the interest of showing a case of intermarriage – Esoueris is a good Egyptian name – in the countryside. But Clarysse also identifies this man as the son of an Alexandrian, Kleandros son of Monimos, who appears as the guardian of one of two Alexandrian women inheriting property in a Greek will from a military settler.[28] This is thus the first known Alexandrian to have married an Egyptian woman.

The second case is that of Stratippos, a Macedonian cavalryman stationed in the Herakleopolite nome, and his son Neoptolemos, who figure prominently in the Zenon archive. Clarysse has identified Neoptolemos' son and grandson, thus the third and fourth generations of this family, in a Demotic self-dedication to Anoubis, a contract in which someone promises the god a monthly payment in exchange for protection against evil spirits. It is thereby possible to see that the younger Stratippos married an Egyptian woman, Haünchis, and their son was named Onnophris alias Neoptolemos, the bearer of a double Egyptian and Greek name. These upper-crust Greek military settlers thus intermarried and were at home in local Egyptian religious institutions.

The third case is a dossier of Demotic surety documents, in which several Greeks appear as village artisans and merchants, living among the Egyptian population. Among them are washermen, a brewer, a farmer, and an oil merchant. The farmer has the double name of Seleukos alias Sokonopis; his father has the good Greek name Pyrrhias, his mother the Greek name Isidora – derived, however, from the Egyptian goddess Isis. These Greeks have business dealings with people with purely Egyptian names, and it seems clear enough that they were fully integrated into the village economy.

From these cases Clarysse draws an important methodological conclusion: The Greek sources almost always give a purely Hellenic appearance, with the Greeks in them seeming to maintain an unaltered Greek culture and life. In the Demotic sources, on the other hand, one gets "an impression of almost total assimilation within Egyptian society." Only the occasional possibility of combining Greek and Demotic source materials makes it possible to get a true sense of the complexity of the lives of these settlers and their descendants, both conscious of Hellenic status (which was officially registered by the government and marked out by some tax concessions) and integrated to a considerable degree into the Egyptian society around them.

In all of these cases, the basic task of putting together scattered evidence is thus complicated by the need to range across the barrier of language in order to do full justice to the reality of Ptolemaic society. In doing so, Clarysse in effect makes the much larger historical point that the view of Ptolemaic Egypt that became orthodox in the postwar period, one of two juxtaposed but separated societies, is at least to some extent the product not only of two bodies of evidence, documenting different types of things, but of the organization of knowledge in the modern academic world, where classical and Egyptian studies are separate branches of learning.

An interesting contrast to this case is provided by a study of the economy of the village of Soknopaiou Nesos by Deborah Hobson. Where Clarysse's article depends on making a small number of telling links across the linguistic divide, Hobson's depends on assembling the evidence of a large number of documents – about 120, in fact – and examining many more (the total documentation of this village exceeds a thousand papyri).[29] Her starting point is a claim by the public farmers of the village, in a petition of AD 207, that the village has no agricultural land except for a tract on the shore of Lake Moeris, the availability of which fluctuated from year to year as the level of the Nile flood affected the level of the lake. When the Nile flood was relatively low, more shoreland was exposed and usable for planting; when it was higher, less was exposed and for less time, allowing it to be used only for pasturage.

Such a claim is very much at odds with the standard image of the Egyptian countryside, in which agriculture is the central activity. If Soknopaiou Nesos had only a few hundred arouras of land at best, and none at worst, how could it survive? Hobson sets out, therefore, to test the petitioners' claim by an examination of all of the surviving documentation from the village. Three types of study are involved. First, all possible references to public or private agricultural land at Soknopaiou Nesos must be examined, to see if they contradict the claim. Second, other references to agricultural activities by the people of Soknopaiou Nesos must be scrutinized to see what they involve. Third, if the hypothesis of virtually no arable land is still standing at that point, other evidence must be adduced to understand what the economic basis of the village might have been.

Hobson pursues all three of these avenues. The first leads to the conclusion that all references in the papyri to arable land at Soknopaiou Nesos can be explained as referring to the shoreland; there was also some limited grazing land. Now this is evidently and essentially an argument from silence; in principle a new document could be published tomorrow attesting land otherwise unknown. But the amplitude of the documentation for this village, all assembled by Hobson, and its chronological spread over a period from the third century BC to the third AD make the argument from silence reasonably compelling. The second investigation turns up evidence that the temple at Soknopaiou Nesos owned land in two or three other Arsinoite villages, and individuals living in the village owned land in at least three other villages. Public farmers of Soknopaiou Nesos worked land in as many as four villages. In all, Soknopaiou Nesos drew on the agricultural resources of at least five other villages, grouped around the lake but at a sufficient distance from Soknopaiou Nesos that something more than daily excursions must have been involved in their management.

The third question takes the inquiry still more broadly into the surviving documentation. A majority of the village population belonged to priestly families, and to the extent that the temple had revenues, these may have helped support the population. It is demonstrable, however, that many if not all of these priests were what we would call part-time clergy, exercising other occupations or economic pursuits. The village also had an important customs station, and it seems that service businesses connected with the traffic passing through this station (particularly traffic in camels and provision of transportation services) were an important part of the local economy. It appears also that some land near the village was usable as pasture for sheep and goats, and turning wool into cloth occupied some part of the population. Fishing on the lake, too, seems to have contributed something to the economy.

The argument so far, then, depends on the exhaustive examination of a large body of disparate material, including especially contracts and accounts, with both negative and positive implications. Hobson concludes by asking if the essentially nonagricultural pattern this study uncovers helps to explain the death of Soknopaiou Nesos in the third century. She suggests that it does, in that the Roman taxation system expected taxes in wheat regardless of the actual output of the village, and that the inability of Soknopaiou Nesos to behave in the fashion expected by the Roman system "is not reflective of a thriving and diversified economy so much as it is an indicator of the approaching demise of the village." This conclusion is evidently of a different sort than the points described earlier, for it rests upon a generalized understanding of the political economy of Roman Egypt rather than upon the documentation from Soknopaiou Nesos adduced so far.[30]

JOINING PAPYRI TO OTHER EVIDENCE

This subtitle may seem hopelessly broad. For present purposes, however, it is meant only to introduce some reflections on subjects that emerge from papyrological documentation but that can be treated adequately only by confronting the papyri with some other class of documentary material, whether written or archaeological. Our first example, in fact, depends on connecting the papyri with the archaeological record. There are various ways of doing this fruitfully. One route is the scientific connection of documents to the houses in which they are found in systematic excavation. Such studies have been undertaken for the ostraka from Elkab, for the ostraka from Mons Claudianus, and for the papyri found at Karanis by the University of Michigan; the latter two are still in their early stages, but one recent article by Peter van Minnen shows already what can be done.[31]

Another type of study is the connection of physical features found in excavations with the verbal evidence of the papyri. A splendid example is an article by Geneviève Husson on the architecture of monastic quarters – "cells" is too humble a term.[32] Husson identifies a whole series of features found in the excavations of the hermitages at Esna and in other monastic sites: storage spaces for dry bread, water-cooling reserves, elaborate kitchens, movable doors, walled-up openings, glassed windows, windowless rooms, storage niches in walls, and so forth. Husson's article was an outgrowth of her dissertation, published a few years later,[33] on the vocabulary connected with private houses in Egypt, and she was thus able to identify the features found at the monastic sites with the terminology found in the papyri. And, by careful study of the papyrological sources for the terminology, she was able to identify many of these features as characteristic of upper-class houses in the cities, rather than of humbler abodes, urban or rural.

The result of the inquiry, therefore, is not merely to put names on the physical features, or to provide physical renderings of words, valuable though those outcomes are. What is more important is that the social character of these monastic hermitages is made clear: these are replicas of the facilities with which wealthy men would have been familiar in their domestic environments before becoming monks. The familiar binary picture of Egyptian monasticism, in which the only choices are the cenobitic monasteries of Pachomian type or the extreme, isolated asceticism associated with St Antony, is thus enriched with a far more nuanced description. In fact, the Polish excavations at Naqlun show us now somewhat less elaborate but also significantly less dispersed monastic habitations, helping again to point to a great continuum of types of monasticism and, we can be sure, of socio-economic levels from which the monks came.[34] Until Husson's article, the archaeologists had ignored the papyri, while no papyrologist had found enough evidence to create a coherent picture. The method is, of course, not a new invention, and it often receives lip service; but it is not often put to use.

We may conclude this sampling by mentioning an article that embodies several themes of this and the preceding section: use of archaeological and epigraphical material, crossing linguistic boundaries, and synthesis based on a large number of documents. This is an extraordinary study by Jan Quaegebeur of the involvement of the Egyptian clergy in the Ptolemaic dynastic cult.[35] In this investigation, Quaegebeur sets out to show that the dynastic cult represented in Egyptian documentation is not simply a Hellenistic ruler cult forced on the Egyptian priests, but a native version parallel to but distinct from the Greek cult. He concludes that "the higher clergy participated actively in the development of their version of the royal cult, which had always been part of the temple ritual, but was adapted to the history of the new royal house." The argument of the article is complex and will not be set out here, but the main components of evidence on which it is based must be indicated.

The state cult of the Ptolemies, which belongs to a well-attested Hellenistic genre, is documented above all in the dating formulas at the start of contracts, in which the yearly eponymous priests of the cults are routinely listed. This is true both for Greek and for Demotic contracts, and the papyrological assemblage of this information has long crossed linguistic lines. The cult in the Egyptian temples, on the other hand, is most strikingly represented in the reliefs and inscriptions (in hieroglyphic Egyptian) on the walls of the surviving temples. These were studied by a paper of Erich Winter, which serves as Quaegebeur's starting point. As in other cases, when these bodies of material are studied separately, they present rather different pictures. Quaegebeur, however, not only brings them together; he emphasizes the importance of looking at several other classes of evidence that help to provide the bridge: cult stelai, decree stelai, statues of sovereigns, and private documents in which the various priests involved appear. These latter include papyrus texts in both Greek and Egyptian, along with hieroglyphic stelai, sarcophagi, and statue inscriptions. The range of material is dazzling, and Quaegebeur emphasizes that he offers only a preliminary exploration and agenda for research. But even in this brief form we are given a good notion of the ways in which these several methodological bents can help to uncover the true complexity of the manner in which the Egyptians responded to and defined their own situation in a state ruled by outsiders.

Chapter 4

Time and place

One of the most fundamental difficulties in working with papyri has already been mentioned briefly in chapter 1. It is the question of what historical reality the papyri refer to. This might seem so obvious as hardly to need discussion, but it is not; rather, it is a major source of confusions – "Confusions," plural, because several types of both error and difficulty arise from it. The common root of them, however, may be summed up in the phrase "in the papyri." Tacitly understood in this phrase are at least two assumptions. First, the world of the papyri (by which, unfortunately, tends to be meant the world of the Greek papyri) is seen as a unity; and second, it is seen as distinct from other "worlds." Both of these are false. The real situation is much more complicated, and this chapter will try to set out several of the elements that drive the historian both to internal analysis of the papyri and to eliciting their connections beyond themselves.

STRATIFYING MATERIAL

Perhaps the most basic and important point is the very simple one that assembled evidence must always be broken down by date and provenance. That does not mean, of course, that there are not aspects of life in which there is continuity over considerable periods of time. Such aspects will be the focus of the section on the chronological axis (see pp. 68–72), where questions of continuity and change over the long run are treated. But if we do not put a stratified analysis in first place, any such continuities will be merely assumed, not demonstrated. Such an analysis, moreover, often has the immediate results of showing that some items of supposed evidence are out of line with the vast bulk of the documents, providing the opportunity for focusing critical attention on their texts. Often enough it will emerge that they have been misread, misattributed, or misdated. There is no substitute for the relentless checking of details. Some discrepancies, however, may be recalcitrant, and their resistance to forced conformity with the rest of the evidence may at times be a valuable clue to inadequacies in the developing hypothesis – or it may only tell us that scribes tended to make certain types of mistakes.

A case in which sorting the evidence by provenance provided the decisive evidence is the starting date of the indiction year in Byzantine Egypt. The indiction was the main method of fiscal reckoning from the reign of Licinius on (AD 312–) and passed into widespread use for giving dates. Indictions came in cycles of fifteen, at the end of each of which numbering began over again; by themselves, therefore, they are as much an irritant as a help to the historian, for a first indiction begins not only in 312 but in 327, 342, 357, and so on. For nearly a century it was believed by papyrologists that the indiction began each year on a variable date, somewhat the way religious holidays like Passover and Easter do, except that no one was ever able to find a cycle controlling and explaining the fluctuation, nor was any other rationale discovered for such a variation.

The principal basis for the belief in this wandering year was a series of dates by month, day, and indiction, to which was added either *arche* ("at the beginning") or *telei* ("at the end"). These occurred with all sorts of dates, mostly (but not quite entirely) in the spring and summer months, and scholars for decades supposed that these meant that the start of the indiction in that year lay at or in close proximity to that date. A related group of texts showed apparent overlaps, that is, dates showing that a new indiction had begun by a particular date when in another papyrus that date belonged to the old indiction.

The theory of the wandering indiction had many logical difficulties of other sorts, but not enough to dethrone it. What led to its collapse was an analysis of the *arche* and *telei* dates that Klaas Worp and I carried out.[1] First, a tabulation showed that all *telei* dates for which the provenance was known came from the Arsinoite and Herakleopolite nomes, whereas the *arche* dates were dispersed over the whole range of nomes from which we had evidence. It thus became clear that these two terms were not twins, but had to have different explanations. A look at *arche*, moreover, showed that its chronological distribution through the year differed from region to region, being much earlier in the Thebaid than in the Arsinoite, and later in the Oxyrhynchite than in either of the former.

A second tabulation looked at a group of texts in which only the hypothesis of an indiction year ending in August, at the same time that the traditional Egyptian civil year ended, allowed the different chronological indexes in the texts to be reconciled. (The papyri of this period often contain other dating elements, like consulates, regnal years, or dates by eras.) The overwhelming majority of these turned out to be Oxyrhynchite, with only a scattering of instances elsewhere, probably for the most part representing errors.

From these two tabulations emerged an analysis that led to an entirely new theory of the indiction, in which different starting dates for the reckoning were used in different parts of Egypt. The Thebaid, thus, used an indiction year beginning May 1 (or the nearby Egyptian Pachon 1) for all purposes; this date corresponds to the official *praedelegatio*, a preliminary distribution of the tax schedule at harvest time. In the Oxyrhynchite, on the other hand, an indiction year beginning with the Egyptian civil year was used for dating purposes, but ways were found of indicating that the fiscal operations of the new indiction had already begun before that date. In the Arsinoite and Herakleopolite, yet another practice is found, in which July 1, the *delegatio* (or final schedule), is used for dating, but the May 1 beginning of fiscal operations is again recognized (hence the use of *telei* in the period from May 1 to July 1). Although new evidence published since 1978 has provided minor modifications to this theory and information about regions previously not documented, it seems fair to say that the movable indiction is not likely to be resurrected.

A similar type of argument enabled John Rea to untangle one of the remaining problems in the year-reckoning of the reign of the emperor Mauricius.[2] By his accession in 582, the habit of appointing annual consuls for the Roman empire had fallen out of use, but the emperor habitually took the consulate in his first full Julian year of rule and counted after that year a post-consular reckoning. Because Justinian had required documents to include regnal years, an Oxyrhynchite scribe might be faced with keeping track of the consular year (starting January 1), the regnal year (starting on the anniversary of accession), and the Oxyrhynchite era-year and indiction (starting on August 29 or 30). No combination of numerals would remain current for more than some months. It was not surprising, then, that by the reign of Mauricius' predecessor it looked as if near-chaos had developed. Mauricius' papyri appeared to show the consular era counted from two different bases, one counting his consulate in 583 as year 1, the other counting his first postconsular year as year 1. Some papyri used one, some the other. This was awkward, to say the least, and a highly uneconomical explanation. But it seemed to emerge from the evidence fairly clearly.

Rea looked at this evidence from the point of view of the date during the Julian year when the two supposed systems were in use, and immediately noticed that the dates using 583 = year 1 all fell from September to December, while almost all of those using 584 = year 1 fell between January and August. From this he argued that Mauricius' consular count, at least at Oxyrhynchos, used a date other than January 1 for the change of the year. Because the apparent regnal anniversary (August 13) is close to the Egyptian civil year, it is difficult to be certain which was used, or if in fact during this particular reign all three were treated as identical. Some difficulties still remain in explaining particular items of evidence, and the situation outside Oxyrhynchos is far less clear. But we see here the results of the simplest of all chronological stratifications, the enumeration by month and day of a small body of material.

Examples could be multiplied, for this kind of stratification is one of the most basic tools available to the historian, but I shall limit myself to two more, similar in kind. It is well known that the Ptolemaic kings had a high-ranking official called the *dioiketes*, often referred to as a finance minister, to whom most of the financial, agricultural, and recordkeeping officials spread throughout the country reported. There is a considerable body of material referring in the Roman period, also, to an official called *dioiketes*, who was an imperial procurator of high rank dealing with matters of financial management. Given the agreement of title, rank, and duties, and given that references to a *dioiketes* are found in every century from the third BC to the third AD, one might well conclude that this office is an element in administrative continuity from Ptolemaic to Roman rule. This is, however, not the case, as Dieter Hagedorn has shown in a compelling study of the office.[3] When the references from the Roman period to the *dioiketes* are broken out chronologically, it is immediately apparent that the earliest secure reference to a procuratorial official is from AD 141, and the earliest possible perhaps twenty years before that. There are, to be sure, references from the period between the Roman acquisition of Egypt (30 BC) and that date, but Hagedorn demonstrates that these are, with one exception, all concerned with lower local officials, who had Greek, not Roman, names and were concerned with relatively minor business.[4] The one exception is the mention of a *dioiketes* as part of the *consilium* of the prefect of Egypt in AD 63, but Hagedorn points out that this man is listed after the military tribunes, in contrast to the later procurator and quite inconsistently with the notion that this could be someone of that rank. The relatively thick documentation of comparable procurators virtually excludes the possibility that a *dioiketes* of this importance could exist but be utterly unattested until AD 120 or 141 aside from the one papyrus.[5]

An unchronological (or even a synchronic) approach to the same data would obviously have yielded a very different outcome, one in which we might agonize over how to reconcile documents that show the *dioiketes* as a high official with those that show him as something much less important. But with the instances put in order, the analysis becomes relatively straightforward. And newer evidence made available since Hagedorn's article was published conforms to the pattern he discerned.[6]

A similar case can be seen in J. David Thomas's demonstration that the offices of *komogrammateus* and *sitologos* were replaced by those of komarch and *dekaprotos*, respectively, during the reign of Philip, between 245 and 247 (though not necessarily simultaneously).[7] It had already been shown by Dieter Hagedorn and Zbigniew Borkowski that the office of komarch was not continuously in use "from the third century BC to the sixth century AD" as it might appear and as had been claimed by standard monographs. Thomas looks closely at the specific documents for the reintroduction of the office (which did not exist in the second century) and shows that the earliest secure attestation is in 247/8, with the *komogrammateus* last attested in 245. A similar narrowing operation puts the last *sitologoi* in 242 and the first *dekaprotoi* in 246. The precise ordering of evidence thus advances the discussion significantly, from simple awareness that these changes occurred to knowledge that they happened in the context of major administrative reforms.[8]

A BROADER MEDITERRANEAN CONTEXT

Despite its centrality as a mode of investigation, analytic stratification of the evidence by date and provenance is only one mode of temporal and spatial contextualization. Side by side with the analytic approach is a more synthetic one, in which the historian asks what is the appropriate framework in which to view the evidence and ask questions about it. Three variations of this question will occupy the remainder of the chapter. All of them are central to the broad issue already raised more than once: how far the evidence of the papyri can be treated as having relevance to something more than a particular period of Egyptian history.

The first of these is the view of Egypt as a part of the social and cultural context of the ancient Mediterranean world, and in particular that world in the Hellenistic and Roman periods. A good recent example is a paper of Marie Drew-Bear, in which she studies the professional athletes and musicians, but mainly athletes, who appear in the archives of the council of Hermopolis Magna receiving privileges – particularly maintenance pensions – from the public purse during the third quarter of the third century.[9] These athletes appear in about 20 percent of the documents of this archive, which Drew-Bear is reediting. At first glance this seems like a high figure, but we know little enough about the manner in which these archives were preserved. This category of document is preserved at Hermopolis alone of the metropoleis of Roman Egypt.

The essential results of the study of these papyri are clear enough. The dominant group of beneficiaries of these civic pensions is the pankratiasts, "heavy" athletes who competed in an event combining boxing, wrestling, kicking, strangling, and twisting (but not biting or gouging). Many of them have the Roman-style triple names (Marcus Aurelius Asklepiades, for example) normally borne by citizens and, more precisely, by citizens whose families received the Roman citizenship before the universal enfranchisement of the Antonine Constitution in AD 212. This pattern suggests origin in the wealthier strata of Hermopolitan society; this is in turn confirmed by the fact that some of these athletes served in important municipal offices and by direct evidence about their landholdings.

If the investigation of these papyri were limited to Egypt, we would be at a loss to provide an adequate context for what they tell us. Studying only Oxyrhynchos, Arsinoe, and other Egyptian metropoleis, we could not tell if the picture derived from these archives was in any way remarkable, a Hermopolitan peculiarity, or something universal. It happens, however, that the institution of civic pensions for athletes who have won first-ranked contests is well known in the Roman East outside Egypt, and Drew-Bear brings a full range of evidence to her examination of the archive. Pliny the Younger deals with pensions in his correspondence with the emperor Trajan, and there are numerous inscriptions, particularly from Asia Minor, referring to them.[10] From these we find, for example, clear confirmation of the pattern found in the papyri: the Asian athletes also largely have the Roman *tria nomina*, not the simple *nomen* Aurelius. They too thus come from families which possessed the citizenship before the Antonine Constitution. Once again, we find also in Asia Minor that some of these athletes served in important municipal offices, including those of annual eponymous magistrate and of moneyer.

The overall picture is profoundly important in establishing that these elements of the Greek culture of Hermopolis in the mid-third century were highly characteristic of the international Hellenism of the period, as we find it in other parts of the Greek-speaking provinces of the empire. By the use of epigraphical evidence, then, Drew-Bear is able to deal a formidable blow to the still-lingering notion that Egypt was still a world apart in this period. At the same time, the comparative evidence helps to clarify the ways in which Hermopolis actually was a renowned source of athletes – a fact noted by the rhetorical author Menander of Laodicea – particularly in the "heavy" sports like the pankration and boxing. It shows, also, that their retirement there after their careers was normal. We learn, thus, both that the overall framework visible in these documents is absolutely typical of the Hellenic East and that Hermopolis occupied an important and distinctive niche in that world.

Egypt was also the site of the most famous learned institution of antiquity, the Museum of Alexandria. Under the Roman empire, the Museum continued to exist, and membership was an honor considered worth mentioning by those who enjoyed it. A number of members of the Museum therefore appear in the papyri, and these cases have raised questions about the nature of the Museum and its membership in this period. Was membership still a sign of high intellectual distinction and activity, as it was under the Ptolemies, or (like the granting of university honorary degrees today) did it include men distinguished in other areas of life, like government service, but lacking in scholarly credentials? The latter was the common view, but from the late 1960s a contrary view began to be voiced, that the "non-scholar" members of the Museum probably had significant scholarly credentials that may simply be unknown to us.

This was the choice of views that Naphtali Lewis set forth in a paper devoted to this question.[11] Although he does not frame his question in quite this way, he takes as his starting point the displacement of the question outside Egypt itself, to the highest level of Roman imperial government. Lewis (1981: 149) sets forth a syllogism he sees at work in the discussion of one exemplary member of the group in question, M. Valerius Titanianus, who held the high imperial offices of prefect of police (*praefectus vigilum*) and director of imperial correspondence (*ab epistulis*): "1) Titanianus was appointed to the office of *ab epistulis*; 2) Only literati or scholars were appointed to that office; 3) Therefore Titanianus was a scholar or literary figure." As (1) is a given, the argument must center upon (2). The implications are, obviously, that if Titanianus must be acknowledged to have had a scholarly or literary dimension, the way lies open to positing such activity for other members of the Museum who, like Titanianus, had public careers – albeit in some cases by no means so illustrious.

Lewis proceeds to enumerate the known holders of the office

of *ab epistulis*. Apart from first-century imperial freedmen, he finds thirty-three individuals, of whom only a third clearly had some literary ability or pretensions that are not simply an avocation. More than half are clearly career public officials, and most of these do not even have any signs of avocational literary interests. The remainder are simply unknown outside their tenure of this particular office. From this, Lewis naturally concludes that literary distinction was by no means a requisite for the office of *ab epistulis*.

The argument then returns to the Museum members themselves, of whom also thirty-three are known. The situation is similar: no more than a third have any known creative or intellectual achievements to their credit, a couple are known only as members of the Museum, and the rest – a clear majority, once again – are attested otherwise only as local or imperial officials or military officers. Lewis (1981: 157) concludes:

> The possibility exists, surely, that behind one or another of these military or bureaucratic exteriors there lurked an aesthetic gift or scientific mind lost forever to posterity, but it strains credulity beyond the breaking point to suppose that that could be true of all or even of most of them.

The point is clear: we cannot attribute intellectual distinction to individuals on the basis of membership in the Museum, and such membership was given also on the basis of other eminence.

In its own terms this argument is unanswerable. It figures here because it takes a problem arising from the papyri mentioning members of the Museum and treats it as dependent upon a problem existing at a higher imperial level; in fact, of course, what is striking is that the characterization of the Museum's membership is not so much dependent on the outcome of the analysis of the *ab epistulis* as it is analogous to it. The evidence is similar, the patterns displayed are similar, and the conclusions are similar. It is hard to avoid the view that the real gain in this case is the discovery that this is not a local question to be solved by analysis internal to papyrology, but a characteristic situation for the world of the empire, to be approached in that broader context. Whether within that setting this is the right answer is another matter. It is by no means evident that the neat distinction of political and intellectual activity is tenable. Certainly it was for the most part the same small elite that carried on both, and the interrelationship of the two looks to be far more complex than the either–or formulation considered here would allow.

PROVINCE AND EMPIRE

The parallelism between the Museum and the *ab epistulis* in the backgrounds of the individuals known to us brings us to a direct confrontation with a particular and central aspect of the connection between the evidence of the Egyptian papyri and the broader spatial context, that of Egypt's contribution to the understanding of the Roman empire as a whole. The majority of the papyri, after all, come from the period of the principate and the late empire. This is not to ignore the similar questions that arise about Egypt's comparability to the other Macedonian empires of the Hellenistic period; rather, it is simply to turn to the Roman period as a more accessible test because of the larger body of evidence from outside Egypt.[12]

Egypt has in fact been a fertile source of material for engaging with one of the major questions of late antique social history, the usability of the evidence of the imperial constitutions compiled in the Theodosian and Justinianic Codes.[13] This legislation ranges over a host of subjects, from imperial administration and taxation to marriage and divorce. Because the compilers of the codes were ordered to omit what was obsolete or redundant, the codes themselves present a very partial picture of the original legislation, but the bulk of material is nonetheless very great. Earlier generations, with perhaps greater confidence in government than most people have today, tended to look on the legislation as an accurate description of reality; that is, presumably what the emperors ordered actually was done. A more skeptical approach in recent decades has looked at the legislation much more as an indication of what problems the emperors felt compelled to address, whether successfully or not. The repeated legislation on some subjects, in fact, has suggested the inefficacy of imperial enactments in these areas. Questions have also been raised about how widely laws sent to officials in one province would have been known and applied in others.

These questions are by their nature unlikely to have a single or simple answer. In some cases, the documentation available to us will probably never offer a sufficient basis for reaching solid conclusions. In others, however, the papyri provide the means to test hypotheses developed on the basis of the codes and to examine the abstractions of imperial legislation to see how far they operated in reality. A good example of the possibilities is provided by a study of several aspects of taxation and monetary history in the fourth century by Jean-Michel Carrié.[14] His starting point is a law of 377, directed to the praetorian prefect of the East, concerned with the collection of clothing for use as military uniforms. The law orders that the annual *vestis collatio*, or collection of clothing, should rest on 20 *iuga* in some provinces, on 30 *iuga* in others. Egypt is specified as one of the latter.

The papyri contain a fair amount of evidence about the collection of garments for military use.[15] Faced with the law, one naturally asks what a *vestis collatio* amounts to, how much a *iugum* is, and whether the rate that results is similar to what is found in the papyri. Carrié invokes an Oxyrhynchos papyrus (*P.Oxy.* XVI 1905), probably to be dated 371/2, often cited in discussions of the subject, and shows that it envisages the collection of a total of 20 garments (11 *sticharia*, 8 *chlamydes*, and 1 *pallion*) on the basis of 1,925 arouras. Bringing to bear epigraphical evidence from Thera discussed by A. H. M. Jones, Carrié argues that the *iugum* was about 96 arouras. The rate in the papyrus would then be 20 garments for 20 *iuga*, and if 20 garments is defined as the standard unit of the *vestis collatio*, the law of 377 can be seen as giving Egypt a reduction in taxes by spreading over 30 *iuga* what previously was collected on 20. More broadly, the papyrus can be seen as the specific application to a particular province of a policy enunciated in broad terms by the central administration.

With this base, Carrié proceeds to look at other fourth-century papyri with rates of taxation (and at compulsory deliveries for reimbursement, particularly of gold and silver). Although the individual documents are often difficult to date and to interpret, he is able to show a common thread running through them of using the *iugum* of about 100 arouras as the basis of taxation, always through translation into local units either of land or of the grain taxes based on land. Undoubtedly future discoveries will modify some of the detailed conclusions he reaches, but for our purposes the underlying pattern is the critical discovery. The imperial legislation that survives marks only one of many stages in the development of the taxation system, but it incorporates a basic manner of setting tax rates at an imperial level that appears to have been consistently used throughout the period. Also consistent is the process of translation of rates set centrally on large units of assessment into rates that can be applied within Egypt at a local level. These certainly varied from nome to nome and year to year, but all of the rates show that the provincial administration set out to convert their overall obligations into rates, based on the actual units of measurement used in Egypt, easily applicable by lower-level tax collectors.

Carrié's article is a good example of linking the Egyptian and imperial contexts through intensive analysis of a small body of material. This is, however, by no means the only way in which such connections can be discovered and demonstrated. For the very beginning of Roman rule, a recent article by Alan Bowman and Dominic Rathbone tackles perhaps the single most fundamental basis for the evasion of Egypt and the papyri by many Roman historians.[16] This is the view, founded on a famous passage of Tacitus,[17] that Augustus kept Egypt in a personal dependence on the emperor and highly centralized rule that was entirely different from the status and administration of other provinces in the empire. From this view it follows that Egypt's institutions must have been fundamentally different from those of other provinces, and that what the papyri tell us about government, public law, or institutions may be ignored when studying the rest of the empire.

Bowman and Rathbone's approach to the question is of necessity wide-ranging and synthetic. The question at stake is clearly not one for which any single document or cluster of texts can provide enough material. The essential contention of the article is that the continuities from Ptolemaic rule, coupled with the Augustan special rules for Egypt, are far less important historically than the Augustan innovations that led to Egypt's ultimate assimilation to patterns of provincial life fully comparable to those in other parts of the Greek East. The continuities from the Ptolemaic period have long been a staple of papyrological writing, but a paper given by Naphtali Lewis at the papyrological congress of 1968 gave voice to a growing sense

that these elements of continuity were far less substantial than
they often appeared, and that the elements of change were
structurally far more important.[18] Bowman and Rathbone did
not have to devote much attention to this issue, relying on the
extensive recent literature already available. Instead, they concentrate on arguing for the minimal importance of the special
rules for Egypt and on the much greater importance of the
Augustan changes. This argumentation, in turn, depends more
on a large body of recent scholarly literature than on direct
appeals to specific papyri.

The essential points about the administration are that Egypt
shed almost all of the characteristics of a monarchy, and the
prefect functioned much like a normal imperial legate; the
administration was redesigned around a series of procuratorial
appointments; many local administrative offices, previously
professional, began to be turned into rotating compulsory
services; the revenues were for the most part destined to the
public treasury; and a typically Roman poll-tax was introduced.
The foundations for a civil society more like those of other
provinces were laid by the conversion of Ptolemaic land allotments to military settlers into purely private land, the introduction of status differentiation and hierarchy into a population otherwise simply defined as "Egyptians" (although it
included many people of fundamentally Greek culture), and
the superposition of a stratum of Roman citizens.

With the creation of these distinctions in the population
began the development of the metropoleis of the nomes into
full-fledged cities. A system of registration of metropolites and
the hereditary transmission of their status was put into place,
with local officials keeping careful records under Roman control. An elite male group within this body was defined around
membership in the gymnasium. And a full structure of officials
was created in each metropolis, posts filled from the elite and
usually strung together in a public "career." Service in these
posts – gymnasiarch, *exegetes*, *kosmetes*, and so on – was an honor,
but it cost the individual a fair amount of money, and the
linkage between private resources and the holding of public
office so characteristic of Greek cities in the Roman East thus
became typical also of Egypt. With these posts the cities increasingly became self-administered, although the full effect of
the development of the elite did not come until the beginning

of the third century, when the cities received permission to have city councils as their governing bodies. Bowman and Rathbone argue, however, that

> the Roman municipalization of the *metropoleis* of Egypt did not begin with Septimius Severus but under Augustus. . . . Already in the Julio-Claudian period the *metropoleis* were to a significant degree functioning and behaving like the Greek *poleis* of other eastern provinces, and by the later second century they were achieving comparable monumental ambitions and administrative responsibilities.[19]

The consequence of this argument is an entirely different view of what the coming of Roman rule meant for Egypt. Instead of a secluded existence under totally different rules, the new rulers brought to Egypt a concerted program of policies aimed at transforming late Hellenistic Egypt into the model adopted elsewhere for Roman rule, in which self-governing cities controlled and managed themselves and their country hinterland, all under the close supervision of Roman magistrates serving for relatively short terms. If this is correct, the historian faced with the papyri is compelled to look at the evidence from Roman Egypt as broadly applicable except to the degree that it needs to be corrected for the stage that Egypt had reached at any given time in its development toward full municipalization. This is perhaps the most fundamental redefinition yet offered of how the historian is to place the papyri in their broader imperial context.

THE CHRONOLOGICAL AXIS

The previous two sections have been devoted to describing some of the potential gains from setting the evidence of the papyri in a sufficiently broad context of place, namely the Hellenistic and Roman Mediterranean worlds. Much that we find in the Egyptian documents can be fully understood only as part of the larger world and through study of the documentation of both other regions of that world and the dominant powers operating in it. But there is another dimension to be considered. If the Mediterranean world is a kind of horizontal axis, Egypt through the millennia is a vertical axis. Enough has already been said about the decisive impact on our picture of Greek and Roman Egypt from combining Greek and Egyptian documents of the same period, but we must turn now to ask in what ways study of Egypt before and after "our" millennium can enrich the historical study of that millennium. A strong plea for this kind of approach was made in an influential article by Deborah Hobson. She adopts the view that

> It is time to acknowledge that Greek papyri from Egypt are not simply a record of relations between Greeks (or Romans) and Egyptians; they are documents of the history of Egypt itself, and as such can only be fully understood in the light of the history of that country, rather than the history of Greece and Rome.[20]

She sets out three reasons for a different approach.

1 The traditional use of papyri suits a preoccupation with political, legal, and administrative questions fairly well, but an interest in social life very poorly. As papyri come predominantly from rural areas, they mainly illuminate questions that are distant from traditional concerns.
2 Much of rural life in Egypt has stayed "remarkably unchanged from the earliest times to the present," partly because of the controlling roles of climate and topography. Knowledge of rural life in Egypt today is therefore of paramount importance for understanding it in antiquity.
3 The written documentation of the papyri has many gaps, whole areas of life not recorded in a "society which was primarily not literate." Other sources are needed to fill in these gaps.

Hobson's prescription comes in two related parts: First, papyrologists need to get to know and to work with colleagues in fields dealing with Egypt in other periods: Egyptologists on the one hand, modern historians and anthropologists on the other. Second, papyrologists need to read as widely as possible in the (usually translated) primary sources and scholarly literature of these other fields. Her discussion stresses anthropology and modern history, mainly because she sees them as able to fill the gaps left by the papyri the most effectively.

There are certainly some difficulties in Hobson's premises. One is that the papyri do not come mainly from villages, as she asserts. Her statement is largely true from the perspective of the

Fayum, where (until the sixth century) the finds are mainly from villages, and particularly villages that dried up. As Hobson's own work has primarily centered on Fayum villages, her sense of the situation is in one sense reasonable. But the bulk of the finds from the Oxyrhynchite and Hermopolite nomes come from the metropoleis of those nomes, above all the vast stock of papyri from Oxyrhynchos itself. And – to follow here the arguments of Bowman and Rathbone described earlier – the life of the metropoleis in the Roman period was decisively impressed with the organizational principles and cultural models of the Greek and Roman world. That is not to say that the metropoleis did not have many characteristics, whole quarters even, of an Egyptian sort,[21] but an approach to them that treats them as overgrown villages comparable to rural Egypt of another era is likely fundamentally to misdescribe them in important respects. This is, I think, the point underlying Leslie MacCoull's argument, in polemical response to Hobson's article, that the broader context in studying late antiquity in Egypt is not Egypt of other periods but late antiquity in the larger Mediterranean world.[22] MacCoull thus emphasizes the geographical axis within the time period.

A second difficulty, perhaps the broader problem of which the preceding point is a subset, is the historian's perennial problem of continuity and change. If it is assumed that rural Egypt of 1100, 1700, and 1988 is pretty much all of a piece, it will become harder to recognize those areas in which change has occurred. The seductive effect of the Egyptian countryside is undeniably very powerful, and the traveller may be hard put to escape the sense of timelessness. A visit to the Fayum in early April shows fields of wheat and fodder crops, the wheat just a few weeks away from the harvest and the fodder already being cut, just as would have been the case in antiquity. Around the edges beans and onions are growing. The canals, with heaped-up ridges of muck excavated from them piled along their edges, the date palms and fruit trees behind mudbrick walls, the little herds of sheep and goats, the dovecotes of mud, all help to give the papyrologist the sense of having wandered back into the second century.

The attentive visitor will, however, see things that jar this antiquarian sensibility. Those piles of reeds and mud excavated from the canals have been piled up by mechanized earthmoving

equipment. Water buffalo, absent from the papyri, are commonplace. A visit in September, moreover, totally upsets the picture.
The fields are full of corn, sugar cane, cotton, citrus fruits,
potatoes, and tomatoes, all postclassical additions – along with,
to be sure, some ancient survivals like castor, sesame, cabbage,
and dates. The land is also full of people, probably at least ten
times as many as in antiquity, a fact that must give a significantly
different cast to the texture of rural life.[23] Other differences
could be noted, but the point should already be clear. There is
a major problem of circularity in any approach that uses the
chronological axis.

That does not suggest abandoning the project, but it does
indicate some of its difficulties. After Hobson's article appeared,
a seminar at the annual meeting of the American Philological
Association discussed three experiments in using anthropological work to help interpret problems in the papyri. One, by
Hobson herself, dealt with naming practices in Roman Egypt
(this article is discussed in chapter 6, below). A second, by
James Keenan, looked at pastoralism. The third, by me, was on
violence. A concluding commentary, by Bruce Frier, pointed
out the theoretical and practical difficulties encountered by all
three papers.[24] Among these are the quality of the comparative
evidence, for anthropological description is also strongly
affected by social and political biases. For example, many of the
examples I cited of village handling of violent conflict are
undoubtedly affected by the fact that, as Frier put it, "Anthropologists are notorious for their vision of pacific societies and
aversion to legal solutions."[25] Frier therefore stresses the possibility of what he sees as a darker view, one in which systemic
violence relies on the threat of force by the powerful against the
weak. This does not seem to me in fact to be in contradiction
with the picture derived from the anthropological literature so
much as to provide a framework for it.[26] But, as both Frier and
I remark, the real difficulty is that the papyri probably do not
offer enough evidence of the right kind to allow the model to
be tested.

Keenan's article is particularly interesting in that it may be
juxtaposed to an earlier study of his on shepherds and village
society in Byzantine Egypt, written six years earlier.[27] The
earlier article sticks far more closely to the papyri, invoking
comparative evidence about shepherds only in two footnotes.

The later one is full of information about sheep and shepherds of other times and places, although it also contains a considerable amount of close analysis of the papyri. What seems to me most striking about it is not that it uses the comparative evidence to answer questions that cannot be answered by the papyri, but rather that the modern material is used to frame questions that do not, unlike those in the earlier article, arise directly out of the attempt to understand the papyri. This function of renovating the questions will be discussed further in later chapters. Frier's response, rather in keeping with the outcome, is in part to wonder – in reply to Keenan's argument that sheep and goats were kept mainly for wool, not for meat – where the meat supply for the cities of Egypt came from.[28]

A significant difference thus emerges between the two axes. The connections of Hellenistic and Roman Egypt with the wider Mediterranean world of antiquity are, in the main, explicable through traditional philological methods of collecting and analyzing evidence, and most of the comparative evidence appears in the forms in which classical scholars are trained to find and use it: texts in Greek and Latin, be these ancient authors or inscriptions on stone. The results, very often, can achieve a high measure of certainty, based on the interlocking character of the evidence. The connections with Egypt – and indeed other Mediterranean societies – of other periods, on the other hand, can only occasionally be elicited by similar methods. One cannot simply describe a pattern in another time and place and interpolate it into the silences of the papyrological record. More often, an indirect approach is necessary. The comparative material makes it possible to frame hypotheses, which may or may not then be capable of testing against the papyri. This process will be explored further in chapters 6 and 7. For the moment, it will be enough to point out that the differences between these two axes correspond to a large degree to the worlds of the documented and the undocumented in ancient society and are thus matters of structure, not accident.

Chapter 5

Quantification

Historical studies in the twentieth century have been profoundly influenced by the introduction of quantitative analysis. For premodern periods this is particularly evident in the insistence of the *Annales* school on the fundamental importance of statistics in establishing the contours of demographic, economic, and social life. Crunching the numbers has been central to all levels of analysis, from the *longue durée* to short-term trends. Not all historians, even within the *Annales* school, have been receptive to such quantification, which is essentially an application to history of methods derived from the social sciences, and some have criticized the possibility that statistics may be used to give history the air of a natural science and thus fundamentally misrepresent its character.[1] Provided that excessive claims are avoided, however, probably few historians today would deny the obvious point that some types of historical questions can be studied only with a quantitative foundation.

For historians of antiquity the use of statistics has been still more problematic, for many have been skeptical of – even hostile to – the notion that meaningful statistics can be had for the ancient world.[2] This reservation is, generally speaking, well founded when it comes to the figures given in the ancient authors, for – even where they have escaped corruption or distortion in transmission – these are often apparently no more than guesses, and they rarely if ever form a coherent set allowing comparison and the determination of central statistical tendencies. In a broader sense, however, such a dismissal would be rash and superficial. Both in the authors and in ancient documents there is actually quite a lot of material capable of quantitative analysis, especially for the period of the

Roman empire.[3] But I emphasize that this is *material for such analysis*, i.e., the raw data from which numbers can be constructed, not the numbers themselves. It therefore generally requires a considerable amount of work of collection and analysis in detail, and no one who has done this kind of work can be unaware of the many difficulties entailed.[4] The papyri offer particularly rich possibilities for such work. They contain vast numbers of figures, for one thing, some of which are at least superficially of a statistical nature, some of which are raw bits of data. And they are themselves sufficiently numerous to furnish all sorts of other raw data capable of quantification. Papyrological historians recognized the potential of their sources many decades ago, and the literature is full of collections of data and analysis of them. It is fair to say, however, that most of this work was of a low level of quantitative sophistication. In particular, little serious attempt was made until recently to look critically at the significance of the numbers derived from quantitative analysis.

These numbers, in fact, are not problem-free. For one thing, in no case do we have, or will we ever have, anything remotely resembling either complete data or a random sample of them. The reasons for this lie in the circumstances through which the papyri have been preserved, which are described in chapter 2. That situation is not irretrievable, but it forces us to ask in every case to what degree the picture presented by the existing data is influenced by the pattern of finds. The most obvious kinds of distortion are of time, place, publication, and milieu. For example, if a tabulation showed that most texts of a particular type were dated to the second century, no meaning could be attributed to this fact without considering how large a proportion of *all* texts were datable to the same period. A statement like "In Oxyrhynchus, literary papyri clearly peak in the early Roman period, whereas in Hermopolis the material is more evenly spread out over the early and later Roman periods"[5] has no statistical meaning. It is only a description of raw data. It *could* turn out to be significant of something, but only study of the chronological distribution of overall papyrus finds from the two cities can begin the task of assessing the significance of the raw data.

The absence of a random sample is, however, not always important. Where a broadly applicable characteristic of the *longue durée* is at stake, for example, temporal stratification of the evidence may be of minor importance and even geographical distribution may not matter very much. An instance of this kind is described in the section below on Demography (pp. 82–5). More commonly, though, other perils lurk. Data may be typical of only a particular type of setting, and even though they have statistical validity for that setting their extension to other milieus is subject to considerable caution. This is the case with the analysis of landholding patterns described in the section on Patterns of Land Ownership (pp. 75–80), where considerable confidence may be placed in the results obtained for each data set, but where the comparison of these data sets opens up a new range of questions. Similar questions arise in the section on Textile Production (pp. 80–1), where a single document can be used to extract important information about textile production in Oxyrhynchos during a very brief period, but where its scalability is very questionable.

The most desirable solution to many of these difficulties is that sketched by Marc Bloch: Many different data sets must be compared, in order that the inevitable errors may cancel one another out, "for it would be extremely unlikely that they should all tend in the same direction."[6] Unfortunately this is only occasionally possible for antiquity, even with the large volume of information available in the papyri. A less satisfying but more often applicable approach is a careful analysis of the influence of find patterns on the evidence and a sifting out of the possible effects.

Another difficulty in developing quantitative information is simply the unreliability of some raw material. The historian cannot assume that the editor has read all of the numbers correctly, particularly because most editors are not very interested in quantification and because numbers are sometimes hard to read. Readings need to be verified and calculations checked before the results can be incorporated into higher-level analysis.

PATTERNS OF LAND OWNERSHIP

Despite the limits, there are cases in which Bloch's dictum is applicable, and we shall begin with an important example. One of the most revealing aspects of any society is the distribution of wealth.[7] In the case of the ancient world, it is preeminently the equal or unequal manner in which land ownership was distributed that determined how stratified wealth was. Land, moreover, occupied a unique position in the economy and government of the Roman empire, in both a practical and an ideological sense. The great bulk of taxation fell on the land, and almost all of the burdens of public service in the cities were attached to the larger landholdings, those in the villages to smaller but still significant holdings. That these disadvantages of land as a form of wealth were insufficient to deter the elite from desiring land is in some measure the result of the enormous ideological preference that all of classical antiquity attached to land as a form of wealth, an ideology connected in some measure to the relative stability of returns from landed property compared to other, more volatile, forms of wealth.

It is the official preference for land as a basis of taxation, however, that gives it a place of honor in the study of the distribution of wealth. The need for an accurate basis of taxation led to the creation of detailed records of landholdings, records which probably did not exist for any other type of wealth. It is only rarely, however, that complete enough examples of this type of evidence survive to allow even the beginning of a quantitative approach to this problem. One of these rare cases is the land registers republished in 1978 by P. J. Sijpesteijn and K. A. Worp[8] and analyzed with care by Alan Bowman in a fundamental article.[9] These list the holdings by residents of Antinoopolis and of one of the four quarters of Hermopolis throughout the entire Hermopolite nome, with the very important exception of the *pagus* nearest to the metropolis. Bowman remarked (1985: 151), after studying the distribution of land in these registers of *c.* AD 350, that

> the very high degree of inequality of distribution of land is certainly significant and seems to contrast quite markedly with such evidence as is available for other places and other periods in the Roman empire. . . . What our Hermopolite lists will not allow us to do, however, is to fit the evidence for the town-dwelling landholders into a picture of the landholding pattern of the nome as a whole, in which as much as three-quarters of the land may still have been held by village residents. . . . There is no means of telling whether this land

was divided much more equally between large numbers of relatively poor landholders in the villages or whether the village pattern displayed a similar degree of differentiation (which one would expect to occur over a smaller range of wealth).

The statistical test used by Bowman for measuring inequality of landholdings was the Gini index, generally represented as R in equations. The Gini index itself provides only a handy single-number summation of the Lorenz curve and permits quick and simple comparison of a wide variety of different data sets. The Lorenz curve, the more fundamental measure, is described by plotting cumulative percentage of (in this case) ownership of property (on the y axis) against cumulative percentage of persons (on the x axis). On this scale, perfect equality would be expressed by a diagonal line from southwest to northeast, showing that 10 percent of the population owned 10 percent of the property, 50 percent owned 50 percent, and so on. Perfect inequality would be represented by a line running horizontally along the x axis to the right end, at which point a vertical line would rise, showing a population in which one person owned all of the property. The Gini index then computes the amount of actual inequality as a ratio (expressed as a decimal, e.g., .753) to a hypothetical state of total inequality. Zero would thus be perfect equality, 1.0 complete inequality.

Bowman's application of this test showed, as he notes, an apparently extraordinarily high Gini index for landownings of residents of Hermopolis, which he computed as .815. The difficulty Bowman faced, as he indicated, was providing a context for this number and the others he derived from the land registers. This is what my 1992 article sought to do. Such context can come both from other ancient figures or from modern ones, and I adduced both. But comparisons are not simple, both because of some inherent characteristics of the Gini index (for example, it usually rises as one moves to higher orders of entities measured, as from a province to a country) and because the data sets on which one may compute the index vary in nature. For example, virtually all ancient data usable for such computations come from lists of some kind, and those lists by their nature exclude the zero cases, persons who had no landholdings at all. The Gini index thus refers to a subset of the population that did own property, not to the entire population. (The index would be still higher if the zero cases were added.) There are four other sets of data from Egypt that I have found usable for comparative purposes. The first is a land register of AD 216 from Philadelphia in the Fayum, in which all owners of private land in that village are listed with their holdings. The Gini index for that population is .516, but an important distinction must be observed: the Hermopolite index reflects total landholdings of a portion of city residents over the entire nome (except one small district), while the Philadelphia register includes the holdings of both village residents and city residents in a single village (the villagers alone have an index of .518). A further complexity, probably more important, is that the Philadelphia list includes only private land (both grainland and orchards); public land is not included, and it is a reasonable bet that this land, leased out, was held in much more equal parcels than the private land, which was presumably acquired by inheritance and purchase.

A second comparative set of data comes from the land registers of late second-century BC Kerkeosiris, also in the Fayum. There we find a lower Gini index (.374). This population includes both allotments to military settlers and crown land, and the data are virtually complete. It is thus partially comparable to the Philadelphia villagers' separate index, but could be expected to be lower as a result of the inclusion of royal land leased to peasants. The crown would have leased to any individual no more than he could work, and the range that one person could work cannot have been very large.

A third data set comes from the taxation reports of AD 308/9 from yet a third Fayum village, Karanis. Here we have all land (the holdings are computed back from tax payments but are almost certainly accurate within a few percent) and all owners, in a particular village. For the small number of urban land-owners the Gini index is .638; that for the village residents is .431. The most obvious comparison for the latter figure is Kerkeosiris' .374, which is relatively close.

Finally, a fourth and somewhat more difficult data set comes from the Upper Egyptian village of Aphrodito around 525/6. A register listing a class of land mostly, if not entirely, owned by urban residents and institutions shows a Gini index for

individuals of .623, a number strikingly similar to that from
Karanis for urban residents owning land in the village.
The comparisons drawn from modern data help to give a
sense of ranges and problems more than they give direct
parallels. For example, land acreage in Wisconsin in 1860 had
a Gini index of .400; a century later it stood at .360. These
numbers, like those from Egypt, exclude zero cases, and they
are obviously very similar to those from Karanis and Kerkeosiris.
Similarly, various modern figures suggest that urban distribution of wealth was considerably more skewed than rural.[10] Most
modern data, however, are for income, which tends in modern
societies to be distributed much more equally than assets
(largely because the percentage of income derived from assets
like land has declined markedly in a wage- and salary-based
economy). The modern country with the highest Gini for
income is Honduras, with a Gini of .630 – hardly a high figure
compared to the Hermopolite index, of course, but relating to
income, not landholdings.

Though there is much we cannot know, then, analysis and
comparison of a group of ancient and modern data sets allow
us to discern a reasonable convergence. What we find is not so
much that the numbers are identical, although some are close,
but that a set of measures of inequality spread over an apparently wide range can, when examined carefully in light of the
nature of the data included, fit reasonably into a single economic and social system. The villages had a broad base of
landholders with a relatively equal distribution of land and,
probably, wealth and income. Inequalities were not eliminated
by any means, but most landowners had enough land to support
a family, and there was a broad band of middle-range men
capable of bearing public obligations. The distribution certainly
varied from place to place and was less egalitarian in the more
attractive (lower-taxed) land than the less attractive, but differences kept within a fairly modest band from about $R = .375$
to .525, roughly comparable to Wisconsin in 1860. The degree
of concentration manifested in the Hermopolite urban population's ownership of land may thus seem in context less
extreme than it otherwise would. Perhaps the most striking
feature of all, in fact, is the absence of really great landed
fortunes in the hands of members of the curial class, fortunes

that might support a rise from municipal status to the aristo-
cracy of the empire.

TEXTILE PRODUCTION

An extensive – nearly a meter wide – but poorly preserved
account from Oxyrhynchos was published in 1979 as "Accounts
of a Laundry (?)" (*P.Oxy.Hels.* 40). It takes only a glance at the
plate to realize just how difficult it was to extract any reliable
text and coherent information from the papyrus in its fragmentary condition. In it is an account of various types of
garments, with numbers of items and amounts in money. The
editor suggested a number of possible interpretations: these
accounts "could concern the weaving, the sale, the fulling, the
dying, the washing, or some kind of tax." In eventually deciding,
with reservations, in favor of a laundry, he raised concerns
about the large numbers of garments and the very imprecise
categorization of these garments.

In an interesting article published in 1986, Peter van Minnen
argued that this account concerned instead exports of finished
articles of clothing from Oxyrhynchos, and that the amounts of
money it records are customs duties on these clothes.[11] Van
Minnen seized on exactly the critical point that had deterred
the editor from viewing this as an account of clothing produced
or sold, the remarkably high volume: nearly 2,000 garments in
a period of five to seven days. Annualized this would lead to a
figure of about 100,000 garments (or even more, if this is a
figure for five days), and because the figures appear to be only
for export, one would have to imagine some production for
local use as well.[12]

We naturally ask whether this is a credible figure, and what
potential sources of error there may be. On the first point, van
Minnen equates these 100,000 garments with about 15,000 to
20,000 large pieces of cloth from the loom. This is approximately on the order of magnitude of garments produced by
Leiden in the second half of the fifteenth century. Leiden had
at that time about 14,000 inhabitants, less than half of what I
suppose to have been the probable population of Oxyrhynchos
in the Roman period. Because our other evidence for Oxyrhynchos does not suggest a town completely dominated by
textile production and export, a ratio equivalent to that of

Leiden would be cause for concern. But a rate perhaps half that of Leiden is at least not inherently implausible – provided, that is, that one accepts the possibility that at least some ancient cities were serious manufacturing centers. This last is a highly controversial point in the study of the ancient economy, but it would be unwise and circular to exclude the possibility a priori. This is perhaps a satisfactory response to the question of credibility. About possible sources of error, van Minnen (1986b: 93) concludes,

> Men are no grapes [he has been talking about production of wine jars in the preceding paragraph], they need clothing throughout the year, not only in Hathyr: so I do not see any reason why the value of the 1.956 figure for one week . . . should be impaired by any seasonal or other influence, as yet undetected.

This is no doubt too simple. For one thing, 55 percent of the garments are for children. This exceeds by a considerable margin the percentage of the ancient population under the age of 14, or even under the age of 19. We must, therefore, reckon either with a local specialization in children's clothing or with seasonal variation in the proportions of adults' and children's clothing produced. Furthermore, we know that Nile shipping was not seasonally uniform. Although it is impossible to offer any precise means of calculating the effect of the Nile's level on the number of garments shipped, it is at least very possible that some months saw significantly lower amounts than others. Moreover, we know that the modern clothing industry is highly seasonal. This may not have been true in antiquity, but it seems unreasonable to exclude the possibility without study.

From all of this we must count as gain at the very least the raising of the question whether large-scale textile production and exporting may not have been a big component of the livelihood of some cities of Roman Egypt. Even if one must discount for seasonality, it seems unlikely that van Minnen's estimates are wrong by a factor of more than 2, and even that yields an order of magnitude in production that must lead us to rethink many of the primitivist assumptions about the ancient economy. The use of quantitative analysis here also allows the formation of a whole set of more precise questions to be kept in mind as we look at and for other evidence.

DEMOGRAPHY

The first two examples of quantification have required the intensive exploitation of a few documents – large land and tax registers in the first case, a single customs-house register in the second. For some questions, however, compact sources of this sort cannot effectively be brought to bear. That is not necessarily because they did not once exist (although the section on religious conversion (pp. 85–9) will consider an instance where they certainly did not). The demographic characteristics of the Egyptian population are a domain where large-scale records on which analysis could have been based once did indeed exist, the population registers assembled by the Roman authorities that included all inhabitants of particular communities. A large enough run of these would be of extraordinary value. But we do not have them. A certain number of first-century village tax lists do survive, but these include only males of taxpaying age (14 and older). They are therefore of some use in analyzing the age-specific mortality experience of adult males, but for other demographic questions they are not helpful. They thus can serve as a check on information from other sources, but not as a primary basis for analysis.[13]

A far more useful source of information is the approximately 300 surviving census returns from Roman Egypt.[14] These originally contained extensive information for each member of a household about name, sex, age, relationships, and in some cases occupation and tax status. Clearly a large enough and random enough sample of these declarations would allow for a very rich analysis of the entire Egyptian population, particularly if data capture in the original census was complete and accurate. Unfortunately, all of these conditions fail. The sample is only about .0016 percent of the original body of material;[15] many of the declarations are only partially preserved; clearly some persons were never registered, most likely persons at the bottom of the social scale; there are reasons to believe that the data are not complete and accurate at times; most of the declarations come from a single century (AD 103–201); about three-quarters of the surviving declarations come from two nomes (the Arsinoite and Oxyrhynchite); and the proportion of declarations from the cities (excluding Alexandria) is considerably larger than any possible estimate of their share of the population.

This description might well give the impression that the situation is desperate. But this is not entirely the case. The database is large enough to give some statistical confidence in conclusions derived from its entirety, although that confidence drops precipitously when subsets are examined; the declarations include enough persons of very humble status to suggest that the social bias is not too marked; age-rounding and age-exaggeration are minimal, much lower than in many modern populations; there is no reason to think the main demographic characteristics of the second century were significantly different from those of other centuries in antiquity or the population of the Arsinoite and Oxyrhynchite greatly different from those of other districts; and the urban bias can be arithmetically corrected. In the end, the major difficulty is simply the lack of a large enough body of complete declarations for a higher level of confidence. The use of a body of separate items of evidence, rather than a single source where data were already assembled in antiquity, thus does not in itself prove to be a difficulty.

The limited quantity of data, however, would prove a grave obstacle to their interpretation, especially because of its jagged distribution, were it not for the existence of comparative evidence. We know a great deal more about many other populations, even premodern ones, than about Roman Egypt. From the information about these other populations demographers have constructed model life tables, showing survival and mortality rates in abstracted form when variables like growth rate and life expectancy at birth are set to particular, arbitrary figures. The plural "tables" must be stressed, for there are several different models derived from different, regionally based, assemblages of data. The models are not a perfect representation of any one population, but a depiction of the typical distribution of an average population within a class. When our data for a population cannot be fitted to any known model at least approximately, there is a fair chance that something is wrong with the data.

The model thus offers two critical benefits in dealing with a population like that of Roman Egypt. On the one hand, it provides a mathematical expression of the behavior of the population to which the data should approximate, and thus helps elucidate the underlying trends partly masked to the eye by the uneven chance distribution of data in a relatively small set. On the other, it allows the investigator to see quickly where there may be real problems in our data, when they are irremediably out of line with the model. In neither case is one freed from the need for careful analysis and thought, but that analysis is structured by the external model.

When the information from the census declarations is subjected to such a scrutiny, it stands up as a whole fairly well, and this is a considerable part of our confidence in the results. The age distribution of females over the age of 5 in the declarations, for example, shows fairly close conformity to the model which assumes a life expectancy of just over 20 years at birth.[16] But equally there are aspects in which the data raise serious questions. The most serious of these is the ratio of males to females, which varies in a fashion entirely incompatible with models and, indeed, with any plausible scenario. The value of the model here, obviously, is to expose difficulties in the data, and these in turn lead to the development of hypotheses to explain the state of the data; these involve the failure to report some males and a tendency to migration. Here the conclusions are far more tentative than they are with female mortality. But the lists of male taxpayers mentioned earlier display similar patterns, as it happens, showing that the problems occurring in our data from the declarations are not just chance artefacts of inadequate documentation but reveal some underlying social phenomena.[17]

The problems posed by statistical study on this kind of basis are evidently qualitatively different from those arising out of the large registers that formed the basis of the two previous sections. In those cases, the computations and statistics themselves were relatively simple and posed few problems. Difficulty arises from interpreting the nature of the registers themselves and their data, but above all from assessing the relationship of the quantitative information derived from them to such information from other times and places and to the general social context. With the census declarations, much more complex questions arise, requiring the use not only of the mathematical models described above but of statistical methods to test theories about the data. Among these are tests of significance dependent on both the data-sample size and the degree of difference between multiple independent samples and tests of the strength of association between two sets of figures.[18]

Despite the difficulties, reservations, and procedures involved in using this body of data, we can fairly describe the investigation as one based on explicit bits of information intentionally collected by the ancient authorities and provided by the people. The role of inference in establishing the data base on which this study was based was relatively modest, limited mainly to elucidating family relationships where these were not explicitly stated and to interpreting fragmentarily preserved declarations. The Roman authorities *wanted* to know most of the things we want to know, like age, sex, status, and relationships, even if their purpose was to tax and control people rather than to model their mortality, nuptiality, and fertility. There are many other classes of data for which information was collected explicitly, particularly involving such things as prices and taxes. But there are also subjects approachable only by asking of the ancient evidence questions it was never designed to answer. The next section deals with a difficult example of this type.

RELIGIOUS CONVERSION

The process of the Christianization of the Roman world was already controversial in its own time, and at least since Gibbon's *Decline and Fall of the Roman Empire* it has been a central preoccupation of historians studying late antiquity. Hardly any view about any important aspect of it is universally accepted, both because the subject stirs profound feelings in both Christians and non-Christians – often divergent even inside these groups – and because the source material, though abundant, is almost all partisan.[19] Both Christian and pagan writers had apologetic reasons to be less than candid about the numbers and identity of their forces at various times and places, and there is no reason to suppose that anyone actually had very accurate information on the subject, for there is no sign that data about religious affiliation were collected in antiquity. Moreover, perhaps the one universally agreed-upon conclusion is that the process varied considerably from place to place.

It was in the hope of providing a perspective not filtered through the ancient authors that I launched some years back an explicitly "preliminary exploration of a new approach," trying to *construct* a body of evidence suitable for quantitative analysis.[20] The word "construct" is appropriate because the evidence was not explicit in the documents, after the manner of sex and age in the census declarations, but implicit. The evidence in question was that of personal names, and the investigation began from the visible transformation of the onomastic repertory of Egypt in the period from the third to the sixth century. The suitability of the onomastic transformation for such analysis was based on two observations: (1) A large proportion of the names in use in Roman Egypt were derived from the names of Greek and Egyptian gods and thus in principle marked an explicit devotion on the part of the name-giver to a particular deity. The local character of cults in Egypt is thus reflected in the local character of nomenclature. Although it is impossible to know in most cases whether specific name-givers (normally the parents of a newborn child) were simply following family or local tradition or acting out of personal piety, there is a fair body of evidence suggesting that at least some were conscious of the religious dimensions of their act. (2) Most of these names pass out of use during the course of the fourth and fifth centuries, with the exception of a certain number kept because they were the names of famous Christian martyrs and thus remained acceptable. For the rest, the onomastic repertory was transformed with the addition of Old and New Testament names, names of apostles and martyrs, and abstract nouns and adjectives for virtues. The resultant amalgam dominated name-giving in the Christian East for more than a millennium to come and is still very visible in orthodox areas like Russia today.

It seemed reasonable to suppose, then, that the pace at which the new name repertory replaced the old would bear some relationship to the pace at which the population of Egypt became Christians. A similar method, and the inspiration for my study, had been carried out for conversion to Islam in medieval Iran, based on medieval biographical dictionaries.[21] But there were no ancient biographical dictionaries for late antique Egypt, nor for that matter any modern prosopographical tools for the period except for one nome (the Arsinoite), and that for only the sixth–eighth centuries. The very imperfect solution was to use six assemblages of material: (1) The Karanis tax lists from the early fourth century; (2) the Hermopolite land registers from the middle of the century; (3) The Abinnaeus archive, dating to the period 342–51; (4) a

Hermopolite village tax list from (as I then thought) 388; (5) the Arsinoite prosopography mentioned above; and (6) a volume of texts from the Upper Egyptian village of Aphrodito at the beginning of the eighth century. In each case figures could be compiled for the names of the persons mentioned and for their fathers (because patronymics are commonly given in the papyri), thus in a sense capturing two generations from each body of evidence.[22]

The actual analysis involves various complexities that may be left to the side here, as may the specific results, in the interests of focusing on the questions of method at stake.[23] But one exception must be made, because it was the focus of part of the critical discussion that followed. Because of the persistence of some pagan theophoric names (mainly as martyrs' names, but this cannot be assumed in all cases) and the use of some "neutral" names (neither pagan nor Christian), the number of Christians is certain to have been higher than the number of persons bearing Christian names. Two arguments converged to lead me to a rough figure of 1.5 as a multiplier (that is, to be multiplied times the number of persons with Christian names to get the number of Christians): (1) Persons with identifiably Christian patronymics but without Christian names themselves amount to about half the number of those with Christian names; (2) Persons with identifiably Christian names amount to roughly two-thirds of the population in the later evidence, sixth century and later, when everyone agrees that Egypt was virtually entirely Christian.

The one serious attempt to criticize the bases of this very tentative approach to a difficult question was an article of Ewa Wipszycka (1986), who was troubled by the fact that my conclusions pointed to a much faster pace of Christianization than did her reading of the literary sources. Part of her discussion concerns questions of the data – the identification of particular names as Christian or not, the dating of particular bodies of evidence. She expressed various reservations, but concluded that they probably would not have a material impact on the outcome. The second part of her discussion starts to touch on points of method, for she attacks the use of 1.5 as a multiplier, arguing that there was no reason to believe that this was as applicable in the fourth century as it was in the sixth, because in the sixth century Egypt was thoroughly Christianized. Finally, she argued that there should be, in the fourth century, a time-lag between the growth of the Christian proportion of the population and the growth in the giving of Christian names to children. These objections were presented by Wipszycka as directed against the *method* of my study, but only the second and third ones were in any sense methodological, and she herself seemed to accept the method in principle. The most serious point of any methodological import was certainly the third, because it called into question the linkage between religious affiliation and onomastic preference that underlies the entire investigation. It did so, however, only in the matter of timing, not of the phenomenon itself.

In replying to Wipszycka,[24] I pointed to the evidence of Christian patronymics in the fourth-century documentation, mentioned above, as an indication that the multiplier of 1.5 was not an arbitrary choice in working with the evidence from that period. More importantly, I noted that her third point, if true – and this is a speculative point about mentality, after all, for which there is no clear evidence – would in fact mean that the number of Christians was *higher*, not lower, than that pre-supposed by the use of a ratio derived from the patronymics, because it would mean that the number of unidentifiable Christians was higher than I had thought.

Wipszycka (1988) returned to the subject in a brief appendix (added in proof) to a long article based largely on Christian literary sources. She did not come back to reargue any of the points raised in her first article,[25] but stated that she was not sweeping enough in her first article: "In my opinion, the data furnished by the papyri scarcely lend themselves to statistical investigations." It is not clear if this is meant generally or with respect to the particular question of conversion, but as it follows a discussion of the inadequacies of the documentation that I had used in the original article, and as Wipszycka offers no reason (other than an admitted dislike of numbers) to shun quantitative analysis generally, I assume the latter.

The points she makes have in fact no bearing on whether the method is usable *in principle*, or whether it is usable on the *type* of material offered by the papyri, but rather on whether the documentation that we have is sufficient in quantity and quality to put the method to valid use, and these are important points.

Wipszycka argues that (1) the number of bodies of evidence is small; (2) their preservation is a matter of chance and their information is incomplete; (3) nothing proves that the rhythm of conversion was uniform throughout Egypt, and the contrary is more likely; (4) even a prosopography of fourth-century Egypt would not ameliorate the situation very much, because of the inadequacy of the data. One could summarize Wipszycka's argument by saying that the situation is likely to have been variable, and that the number of data points needed is therefore larger than what we have or are likely to have.

These are difficult questions, not soluble by simple statistical tests, but they ask essentially how much confidence one may have in the results obtained from these data.[26] The answers might theoretically run from Wipszycka's apparent "none" to the opposite extreme. In the original article I did not quantify my own confidence level, and indeed I expressed my own reservations about how far one could push the results of the inquiry; but my confidence was considerably reinforced by the fact that my analysis led to the view that the pattern of conversion followed an S-shaped curve very similar to that deduced by Bulliet for conversion to Islam. More recently, I learned of forthcoming work on the Christianization of the Roman empire by a sociologist of religion, Rodney Stark.[27] Stark independently deduced from other evidence and from models of modern conversion a curve essentially similar to what I had proposed, assuming a fairly constant rate of growth from a small base. Because Stark's work entails an analysis of the way conversion works, one may be confident at least that something more than coincidence is involved in the convergence of results.

For the moment, I would personally regard the pattern of conversion for which I have argued as a working hypothesis, so far not invalidated by any evidence but rather fitting with what evidence we have and given some weight by its convergence with indications from other times and places – but one with still only a very rough scale of the pace of conversion. To me, that seems to be a useful result, given the intractability of the other evidence for the question, and to suggest that the approach has some value. But it points unmistakably also to the constant need to assess the character and quality of the evidence in all quantitative work, a need that increases as the evidence becomes more indirect and less dense.

Chapter 6

Asking questions

Most papyrologists would probably nod unquestioned assent to the description of the field given by an avowed outsider, Bruce Frier, in his commentary on the seminar on new approaches to the papyri described in chapter 4: "a cautious reconstruction that proceeds document by document, with each new papyrus first subjected to careful analysis as an artefact in its own right, and then linked to the corpus of other surviving papyri."[1] This method is described by Frier as "antiquarian," but he is quick to say both that this is not a criticism of the field and that antiquarian methods must remain central to the field because of the nature of the surviving source material. To it, however, he contrasts interest in a newer set of questions, coming into ancient history proximately from medieval and modern history (especially via the historians of the *Annales* school) and ultimately from the social sciences. These include social structures, behavioral patterns, and ideological currents.

There is, nevertheless, a difficulty in this view, which apparently sees some questions dealt with by papyrologists as inherent to the antiquarian enterprise itself and others as coming from the outside, *and* correlates this division between older and more recent studies. It is no doubt pragmatically true that a scholar faced for the first time with a census declaration addressed to the village secretary, the *komogrammateus*, will naturally ask, "What is a *komogrammateus*?" The basic tendency to assemble information about the vocabulary and institutions exhibited in the papyri does seem to follow almost automatically from the act of editing, as one can see in beginning students of papyrology. But the point should not be pushed too far, for even questions like "What is a *komogrammateus?*" are in themselves largely the natural product of minds trained in particular disciplines, above all philology and law. It was from just these disciplines that most of the pioneers in the field came, and it is not surprising that the sets of questions that come naturally to those trained in nineteenth-century classical philology and in Roman law studies are those on which most of the earlier papyrological literature centers.

The rich stock of monographic literature routinely cited in the notes of editions of papyri is largely the working out of this original project. In a papyrologist's dream world, every office would have a recent monograph devoted to it; so would every institution, every tax, every contract type, and so on. Many of these monographs, it must be admitted, are not very interesting to read, and most of them are undoubtedly cited far more often than they are read. It is as if every text to be edited presents a list of problems, and the editor who finds a monographic treatment of one of them can check it off as solved, requiring no further thought. When everything has been checked off, the document is finished.

This tradition has achieved notable gains and shows no signs of disappearing, as I shall argue in chapter 7; nor should it. One may well argue that this categorical approach is an essential foundation to more adventurous investigations, although it does have two side effects: the first, which Frier pointed out, is that the weight of scholarship tends to dissuade outsiders from entering the enclosure; the second is that it discourages papyrologists from venturing outside, for there are always chores of the traditional sort left undone. But perhaps it is enough here to make the point that the philological and legal approach is – no matter how valuable – not natural or inevitable; it represents a particular kind of intellectual venture.

In this chapter I shall look at some examples of questions that do not come entirely from the papyri "themselves," studied in this philological tradition, but that are raised at least partly outside it, with the papyri then brought in to help test hypotheses formulated from other disciplines or sources. These range from bodies of material well within the traditional subject matter of classical philology to those well without.

OTHER ANCIENT TEXTS

An explicit and self-conscious example of drawing a hypothesis for testing from the study of the literary sources is an article by Jean Gascou on the institutions of the hippodrome – the scene of chariot-racing – in Byzantine Egypt.[2] Gascou begins by invoking the work of Alan Cameron, at that time recently published or about to appear, which had refuted the commonly-held notion of the circus factions of Constantinople and other large cities as political in character.[3] Gascou frames the problem as follows:

> The orientation of Alan Cameron's research and his manner of posing the problems proceed from the nature of his sources. They are essentially literary and fundamentally inform us only about Constantinople and a few other very large cities of the empire, like Antioch and Alexandria. They cover carefully the changes of fortune of the history of the circus and its great events, but they leave the commonplace, daily, and institutional in the shadow. The papyrological sources, an eminently concrete and practical documentation, can give a useful counterpoint for a thesis elaborated, if we may so describe it, at Constantinople.[4]

Cameron's view, briefly stated, is that the *demoi* and *mere* mentioned by the sources in connection with the hippodrome are neither urban subdivisions (of space or of people), nor subordinate organs of municipal government, but the totality of the members of the fan-clubs of the Blues and Greens. Although they were organized in a manner derived from typical Roman professional associations, *collegia*, and thus reminiscent of institutions with legal standing and public recognition, they were not for all that formal political agents of any sort. In Cameron's view, *demos* and *meros* ("part") are interchangeable terms.

As promised, Gascou subjects this view to testing against the data from the papyri. He notes that the introduction of the circus into Egypt is an ideological and cultural aspect of the Romanization and municipalization of the cities, which began (as we have seen) under Augustus and reached a visible stage with the introduction of civic councils under Septimius Severus. His starting point – almost inevitably, when one is dealing with papyri – is the financing of the circus. Between the fourth and the sixth centuries a system of dispersed requisitions and exactions, depending on the compulsory service of councillors responsible for the supply of the circus, had given way to the "fiscalization" of the circus. That is, the financing becomes essentially a public service of the city, executed through taxation and comparable in this respect to the baths. It appears that this full incorporation of the circus into the municipal organization was the result of imperial orders in the intervening period.

What is most striking, perhaps, is that the municipal authorities responsible for supplying the circus establishments show a complete indifference to the distinction between Blues and Greens, that is, to the "factions." They regard the entire circus, rather, as a single entity, with the colors as a derivative element only. And the documentation uses only the word *meros*, "part," to describe the factions. The word *demos* never occurs. Gascou proceeds to argue, from a tax account in a papyrus, that in fact *meros* does have a sense relevant to geography in the cities of Egypt, where the taxes to support a particular color were collected from specific streets: the *meros* of the Greens included particular streets, that of the Blues different streets. But, Gascou demonstrates, the papyrus shows us the *meros* functioning only as an accounting subdivision, and the individual streets are the actual unit of functioning: "It is by a simple act of writing that those who drew up [this papyrus] transformed the payments of streets into payments due to the Greens" (Gascou 1976: 198 n. 2).

Gascou's analysis leads to the conclusion that the term *meros* derives from the financial realm and reflects the unification of the financial support of the circus in the municipal administration with a basis in taxation. He then turns to the *demotai*, the activist partisans of the two colors. As it happens, the term never appears in the papyri with reference to the circus, nor does its root *demos*. But the term *demotes* does appear in the papyri of the Byzantine period, along with a term for leading members of the group (*protodemotes*), and Gascou (1976: 206) argues that "the *protodemotai* of the cities of Egypt [were] the presidents of a subordinate municipal college, located [organizationally] below the curiales, of which the ordinary members were called the *demotai*."

Whether there is any connection between this group and the *demotai* attested in connection with the circus is more speculative. Gascou argues that such a link cannot be excluded, particularly because Byzantine associations were never entirely divorced from the state and free of state obligations. The *demotai* of the cities of Egypt carried a variety of public obligations, and it is not impossible that financing the circus became one of these.

The results of Gascou's investigation, then, may be from one point of view described as supporting Cameron's overall thesis but modifying its details in several regards. The overdescription of the factions as political entities representing social or ideological cleavages in society receives as little support from the papyri as from other sources. On the other hand, the relationship of the circus and the colors to the organisms of the city administration turns out to be a lot more complicated. And here is perhaps the greater value of the study, in that it brings evidence to bear on a range of aspects of the circus that are simply missing in the literary sources. From this point of view, Gascou's work does not so much either challenge or confirm Cameron's thesis as deepen it and provide it with a richer context that takes account of our knowledge of the workings of late antique cities and their elites.

A different but equally interesting case of the papyri playing a role in examining a thesis derived from literary sources is a study by Ranon Katzoff of rules governing the relationship of dowries and marriage gifts in Roman and Jewish law.[5] Katzoff reexamined a thesis set forth by Asher Gulak in 1933 linking late Roman law, some provisions in rabbinic literature, and the evidence of some papyri and inscriptions from Egypt. Gulak pointed to the provisions in Novel 97 of Justinian (AD 539), requiring the husband to make a marriage settlement on his wife equal to the amount of the dowry she or her family contributes to the marriage, as well as to the rule in the earlier Syro-Roman Lawbook that in the West an equal amount is to be given by the husband, while in the East the husband's gift is half that of the wife's. He then connects these rules to a traditional Jewish practice of requiring the husband to contribute an amount equal to half of the dowry, which was in turn succeeded by a requirement that the amount be equal to 100 percent of the dowry.

As Katzoff points out, this thesis has significant implications:

> For the study of Roman law it would demonstrate a specific oriental influence precisely in an institution where such influence has been the subject of considerable debate. For the study of Jewish law it would represent an instance of foreign influence, as Gulak puts it, or, stated more conservatively, an instance where a Jewish legal institution is supported by the practice of neighboring gentiles. For the study of papyrology this would afford an opportunity to assess the degree to which conclusions drawn from papyri found in Egypt are generalizable to neighboring provinces of the Roman empire.[6]

It is evident that a lot is at stake.

Katzoff's examination of the thesis takes several directions. Two of these are independent of the papyrological evidence. First, he argues that the functions of the Roman gift matching the dowry and of the Jewish dowry increase are different. The Roman gift is in principle given at the start of the marriage and intended to specify the husband's "contribution to the wealth of the common household" (Katzoff 1985: 235) or, if made to the bride's family, "to serve as payment for the bride" (Katzoff 1985: 235).The Jewish provision, on the other hand, takes the form solely of an obligation, which is actually to be paid by the husband only as a penalty after the dissolution of the marriage, thus serving in effect as an economic disincentive to the free divorce otherwise available to him. (Penalty clauses with similar intent are also known from Egyptian law.) Moreover, it affects only cash dowries, where the husband receives the use of the cash during the marriage, and it is thus similar to penalty clauses in loans.

Second, the supports for the view that Jewish law eventually required a full match of the dowry by the husband's gift prove to be flimsy. The key passage, in fact, appears to mean instead that in some places the local custom is to write in the marriage contract (the *ketuba*) a dowry amount twice the actual amount, and in such places the groom will receive from the bride's father half of the amount written. "Everyone involved understood that these fanciful amounts were part of the festivities, and they were not taken seriously by anyone. . . . The custom is well-documented in post-Talmudic times, when it understandably caused considerable litigation."[7] This custom thus is in no way parallel to the 50 percent penalty clause.

The 50 percent increase, which was evidently a typical Jewish practice, is an example of a particular type of dowry increase, carried out juridically by having the marriage document assert that the bride's family gave the groom more than was in fact given – not the fanciful doubling, but an amount including the penalty clause. (In the same way, many loans specify a "principal" amount considerably higher than what was actually loaned, as a means of evading usury regulations.) Katzoff completes the circle of the argument by asking if this type of dowry increase by fiction was common in the Roman and Hellenistic worlds. The practice was certainly illegal in Roman law, but the repeated prohibitions of it certainly suggest that it was attempted. In line with this, Erwin Seidl argued that documents from Roman Egypt show specific instances of fictitious dowries which point to its being a frequent practice. Seidl, as a specialist in Egyptian law and Demotic documents, was beginning from the view that Egyptian practice, as shown in Demotic marriage documents, allowed penalties in the case of divorce which could be expressed in this fashion.

The documentary base from Roman Egypt, however, turns out to be three texts, one inscription and two papyri.[8] Katzoff shows, using standard philological analysis, that none of these offers any reason to connect it with a practice of fictitious dowries; in one almost certainly the issue is the prohibition of soldiers' marriages, in another the prevention of fraud. In a third, Seidl's interpretation depends on a reading of the Greek that is grammatically impossible. The basis for arguing that the practice was widespread in Roman Egypt thus collapses. But Katzoff recognizes that this is an argument from silence, capable in principle of being contradicted by new documents. Moreover, it can hardly be expected that the papyri would provide the needed evidence in any abundance, because "if a dowry is fictive, in whole or in part . . . the document can hardly be expected to say so" (Katzoff 1985: 237–8). What Katzoff does, therefore, is not so much to demonstrate that something is untrue as to show that there is no evidence that it is.

The discussion of the papyri thus plays a secondary role in

the logical construction of Katzoff's argument, in part because silence would not be surprising even if the thesis he is combatting were true. Still, the papyri often provide to the attentive reader signs of divergence between norms and practices, and any such signs would be important markers of the real situation in provincial law. The absence of such signs removes any need to interpret Justinian's legislation or the Syro-Roman Lawbook in light of supposed current practices. Although the papyri are only a small part of the argument, then, they are not an unimportant one. More interestingly for us, however, their significance comes entirely from being embedded in a discussion originating in the confrontation of Jewish and Roman legal sources.

Our third example in this section is a study of the lower orders of clergy in Byzantine Egypt by Ewa Wipszycka (1993). The article starts simply from the observation that these ecclesiastical functionaries have had no systematic study up to now (and therefore may be assumed to need one). The evidence for subdeacons, lectors, cantors, and porters (in descending order of rank) comes particularly from canonical literature in the sense of texts setting out church law and regulations. As usual with such texts, they both describe the way things were supposed to work and provide some hints of what problems required legislation. But they obviously have, like all normative writings, serious limitations. Wipszycka supplements their information, therefore, with that from two other categories of sources, hagiographic literature and documentary papyri. Hagiography, as she notes, is designed to edify the reader and thus offers positive or negative models more commonly than ordinary reality.

By now the papyri as a source of just such an everyday reality have become a commonplace, even in this book, although some of their limits for this purpose have become clear. Wipszycka notes that in fact the papyri, though rich in information about the private life of minor orders of clerics – their landholdings, non-ecclesiastical occupations, loans, sales, and the like – tell us relatively little about their ecclesiastical functioning. But in one critical area the documents are vital: they help inform us about the identity and character of the churches to which these clergy were attached, and thus to understand the function they played. They also have some importance in giving us a sense of the relative numbers of holders of the various ranks. The scrutiny of the documentary texts does in fact lead Wipszycka to some important conclusions. One is that the importance of the minor orders declined significantly over the centuries in question (fourth to eighth). A second is that the lector was numerically far the most important office; despite Wipszycka's suspicion of statistics and her great caution in avoiding precise counts here, she recognizes that the predominance of mentions of lectors in the reasonably abundant documentary texts cannot be a matter of chance. A third is that the minor clergy were in the main attached to the larger, principal churches of the cities. Wipszycka in fact links this to the first conclusion, in pointing out that the church of the fourth century was based in a relatively small number of edifices, both urban and rural, gradually over time creating a much more numerous network of village churches of modest size. In the developed church, a large number of small establishments, each with only two or three clergy, succeeded the more concentrated forces of the earlier centuries. The minor clergy still played an important role in providing the solemnity required for festivals in the larger churches, but structurally their role declined.[9]

In this case, then, the role of the papyri is directly complementary to that of the literary sources; they answer a set of questions raised by an attentive reading of the canonical and hagiographic sources but which these are incapable of answering. At the same time, the papyri by themselves would tell us almost nothing about the functions, hierarchy, or relationships of these orders. The richness of Wipszycka's article comes from the linkage of the two groups of sources and their questions. Editors of papyri hardly ever read the ecclesiastical literature, and a straightforward "antiquarian" approach limited to the papyri was always unlikely to yield interesting results on a question of this sort. The sterility of an approach limited to the canonical sources, on the other hand, should be evident.

In leaving this section it is important to point out that there is nothing easy about undertaking the kind of investigations I have described. Particularly in the latter two cases, the ability to pose and analyze questions raised by important bodies of literary material depends on many years – certainly more than a quarter-century, in Wipszycka's case – of investment of time in the study of those sources, which are not part of the standard training of classical philologists and ancient historians. But it is equally clear that some types of questions simply cannot be raised, let alone answered, without precisely this kind of study.

AN OUTSIDE DISCIPLINE MEETS THE PAPYRI

Preceding chapters have repeatedly stressed the iterative and interactive character of the relationship between sources and questions. A good example is provided by the paper of Deborah Hobson that was part of the seminar on comparative approaches to the papyri discussed in chapter 4.[10] This article is in considerable part an exploration of the meaning of names based on *kopros*, dung. The initial interest in the problem stems from working with papyri containing such names; that is, it is in origin a philological "what is this?" type of question. Beginning from Sarah Pomeroy's demonstration[11] that these names cannot be (as was long thought) an indicator that the individual had been exposed in infancy, Hobson looks for an explanation in anthropology, from her reading in which she had noticed an extensive anthropological literature on derogatory-protective naming. This type of naming gives babies negative names in order to ward off the evil eye and ensure the child's survival. Such names would have been particularly common where a mother had had difficulty conceiving or had lost children at a very young age. Is this the explanation in Roman Egypt? Hobson (1989: 165) concludes that "a full understanding of naming practices would require first-hand knowledge of the personal background and circumstances of the individual, a kind of documentation that we papyrologists will never have." Up to this point, then, Hobson has tried to move beyond an entirely negative result derived by philological method to a positive hypothesis derived from another discipline. But the means of testing it are lacking.

Hobson (1989: 174) goes on to argue that "anthropologists are in their own way equally restricted in their sources" because they tend to concentrate on oral culture and do not correlate written and oral evidence. She suggests that papyrologists are well placed to frame questions for anthropologists to try to answer from a combination of written and oral sources, with the hope that the results would then offer truly useful models for interpreting the papyri. Frier (1989), in his response to Hobson's paper, expresses considerable skepticism about the degree to which ingrained, traditional systems of naming actually represent the contemporary culture in any direct way:

> Intuitively it would appear that nomenclature is often highly traditional, unreflectively accepted as a subsystem simply because there is need of order in the naming of persons (as in language generally); whether and to what extent the subsystem initially either incorporates or expresses broader cultural values, and then continues to do so, is deeply problematic.[12]

Actually, quite a lot of change in Egyptian naming practices *can* be demonstrated, and the emergence of the dung-names is a striking example: it is an innovation of the Roman period.

Hobson's own reservations about the method deserve further thought. Despite the attractions of her proposal for collaborative research, it must be admitted that imposing one's own research agenda on others is never easy. There is another route, however, which seems more immediately promising. That is to use the anthropological literature to predict what other manifestations one might hope to observe in the papyri, or in ancient societies generally, of the patterns of which we suppose we are seeing the results. In the case of the copronyms, naming practices are an element of a larger system of belief, in which envy, the evil eye, and demons play prominent roles. Although there is considerable variation in the exact form of this type of construction of reality, it appears with a wide enough distribution in time and space to offer a considerable range of possible accompaniments and consequences that might turn up.

As it happens, there is quite a fair amount of evidence for such a belief system in Greek antiquity, turning up in documentary, archaeological, and literary forms over a considerable range. It is probably a Greek, and perhaps specifically Hellenistic, development, but it affected Roman thought as well. The evil daimon of envy that is blamed for most divorces in the papyri and that turns up in Catullus' Lesbia poems as hostile to happiness in love is certainly a manifestation.[13] In other words, although it may be impossible to confirm the hypothesis suggested by anthropology directly – that is, with specific evidence about the intent of parents in giving a name – it is possible to show that other consequences of the hypothesis are in conformity with evidence we do have. That this falls short of proof is immaterial. We are not generally in a position to prove interesting explanatory hypotheses about antiquity.[14] If they survive all attempts at disproof based on substantial evidence, we have done well.

But have we? One point remains to be noted at the end of this interaction of philology and anthropology. These dung-names are barely attested in the Ptolemaic period; though not an invention of the Roman era, they come into wide use only then. To be more precise, except for a single instance from the first century BC, the names do not appear before the second century AD.[15] The names remain common until the middle of the fourth century, after which they decline precipitously in popularity. There is nothing obvious in the anthropological hypothesis to explain this chronological distribution, for we know that the evil daimon is not a development of around AD 100, nor does it disappear from the popular mentality in the middle of the fourth century. It would be going too far to say that the chronological distribution in itself invalidates our working hypothesis, but it does leave us with a significant challenge to it. For that matter, like other explanations based on mentality or social and economic conditions, it encounters difficulty with the fact that its beginning and end are so precisely fixed; the problem may thus demand a more historical approach than most anthropology has offered.

QUESTIONS AWAITING AN ANSWER

Similar problems are offered, but in a much broader context, by an important article of Edouard Will on the potential usefulness of the anthropology and sociology of the colonial and post-colonial world for the study of the Hellenistic East.[16] Will begins by asserting the necessity for a self-conscious, rather than unthinking, use of perspectives offered by the historian's contemporary world, and argues that the different approaches to the colonial world that have developed in an era of decolonization offer just the useful contemporary perspective needed. He describes the limits of the classic works on the Hellenistic world by earlier historians, culminating in the prewar work of Michael Rostovtzeff and Claire Préaux,[17] which he sees as lacking in a clear approach to the sociological problems posed by the relations between colonizing and colonized. For this reason these accounts showed insufficient interest in the agrarian world, were too much interested in the state and its role, and too much written from the point of view of the dominating power, the Greek settlers and Macedonian rulers. This last defect was reinforced by the lack of any critical self-consciousness about European colonization and imperialism.

In the postwar world of decolonization, western scholars have no longer been able to look at a colonial world with the same "good conscience" they once had, confident that European domination was good for the ruled as well as for the rulers. Will argues that the new vistas opened up by this change of outlook, when coupled with a Marxist-influenced interest in the relations of production, make possible an entirely new approach to the society of the Hellenistic world. In this view, the analysis of states becomes of secondary interest, the relations of Greeks and non-Greeks of central importance.

The avenue that Will describes for pursuing this goal is an explicitly comparative one. If we define the Hellenistic world as a colonial one, then a wide range of colonial and post-colonial zones (in the latter Will includes South America) offer a range of "living societies accessible to more penetrating methods of investigation than the methods proper to the ancient world" (Will 1985: 282). Although Will recognizes the important differences that we must take account of, both among modern colonial worlds and ancient societies, he asserts that accepting the "colonial hypothesis" opens up such a large range of useful modern literature that we can renovate our entire approach to Hellenistic society.

On this basis, Will proceeds to offer three sets of observations. The first is a four-part typology of relations of colonized to colonizers. The second is a pair of important differences between antiquity and the recent past. The third is a pair of illustrative examples in which he believes that the use of comparative material helps to illuminate the situation in antiquity, in particular in Ptolemaic Egypt.

The typology (borrowed from an anthropologist of Africa) sees four main types of indigenous reaction to external domina-tion: (1) active acceptance, most typical among notables intent on retaining power and among those looking to gain power, entailing a considerable measure of assimilation; (2) passive acceptance, usually by far the majority stance, natural among those already in a state of dependence and witnessing no major change in their status; (3) passive opposition, generated in many cases by a high level of anxiety over social and economic change, manifesting itself especially in withdrawal, strikes, evasion, and disappearance; and (4) active opposition, manifesting itself ultimately in revolt, whether spurred by political, economic, or cultural factors.

Will notes that these stages are not necessarily a logical or chronological progression, that they are a theoretical typology that may well vary from time to time and place to place, and that each group can develop internal fissures under various pressures; he cites the tendency of victorious revolutions to fissure between those more ready to adapt the techniques of the foreign dominators and those intent on purifying their culture from such foreign attributes.

The first of the two key differences Will sees is that the conquest of the East by Alexander and his successors was essentially political and military in character and origin, whereas modern colonization was heavily driven by economic interest, whether access to resources or the development of trading networks. This distinction is broadly characteristic of the difference between ancient Greek culture and modern capitalist civilization, in Will's view. The second is that almost all modern colonialism was accompanied by, and sometimes largely executed by, a religious missionary movement, propagating a universalizing monotheistic religion; by contrast, both conquerors and conquered in the Hellenistic world were polytheists, open to the cults of others and not particularly intent on imposing their own on anyone.

We come, finally, to Will's two case studies. The first is the use of petitions addressed to the king in Ptolemaic Egypt. Will wonders if they ever reached their destination and had any outcome. He cites the operation of a Peruvian system of petitions to high officials, in which the petitions generally went nowhere, being perpetually described by bureaucrats as in the course of transmission. During these long silences the petitioners became effective dependants of the bureaucratic office, but acquired in this way the ability to say to others that their case was under official scrutiny. Did the Ptolemaic system work this way, he wonders? The second case study is the impact of the introduction of coinage in a society not accustomed to it, and particularly its use as a medium for payment of obligations to the government. He points out that Peruvians were driven to accept wage labor, especially in mines, in order to earn enough currency to pay the money taxes imposed by the government.[18] Moreover, the actions of the foreign government and settlers tended to turn money into the single standard of wealth, in contrast to traditional local ways of measuring it; this process was ultimately destructive to the local economy.[19] Did the same thing happen in Egypt?

Now it is by no means clear that either of these questions would, if pursued in detail, lead to the conclusion that Ptolemaic Egypt did, in fact, show the same phenomena as colonial or post-colonial Peru (or South Africa, for that matter). Ptolemaic petitions normally do not have a date of submission, but the surviving ones very commonly have an official subscription giving instructions for the handling of the case – which does have a date. We cannot, therefore, measure the time that elapsed between complaint and action.[20] We do, on the other hand, know that at least some petitions received official response, although it is likely enough that the surviving petitions come mainly from recycled official archives composed precisely of petitions that had been dealt with. It would not do for us to assume that the Ptolemaic administration was entirely honest and efficient, but neither do the actual documents give any warrant for a comparison to the Peruvian situation Will invokes. As to money, the Egyptians were very well acquainted with silver, even if largely uncoined, as a standard of value before the Ptolemies. And Ptolemaic taxation in money was relatively light, achieving a symbolic value as much as anything; the bulk of the taxes continued to be collected in kind. It is therefore by no means clear that the Ptolemies created the kind of pressures for their subjects supposed by Will's parallels.

Even this brief analysis is sufficient to show that the parallels may actually produce very misleading views. One may reply, as I think Will certainly would, that the value of the parallels is in formulating questions, not in providing their answers. That is part of the truth, and it is why this set of issues is treated in this chapter. But there is another answer, which seems to me more interesting. The parallels allow the formulation of hypotheses about how certain aspects of Egyptian society in the Hellenistic period might have functioned. Let us suppose that these hypotheses can be not merely called into doubt (as I have tried to do above) but definitely refuted. The value of the negative results is not only that we learn some particular (negative) characteristic of ancient society; rather, it is also that the reasoning leading to the hypothesis can now be unpacked and examined. What fundamental or contingent characteristics of the ancient world, and of the particular society in it that we are studying, underlie and produce this interesting difference between Egypt and Peru?

That point leads me to think that Will should have included a third fundamental point among the differences and caveats to be kept in mind, even if it is not quite of the same type as the other two. It is that categorization, however useful, has sharp limits. This is true of the modern comparanda; 'colonial' is, though a useful category, one that covers a wide variety of circumstances. Like the Greek-centered approaches that Will deplores, it is itself a categorization constructed from the point of view of the colonizer. It tends to obfuscate the enormous differences in social, political, and economic organization of the societies visited with outside domination. Although anthropology has now moved very considerably from its character of a generation ago, its literature – especially that which by virtue of the passage of time has been incorporated into the bibliographic consciousness of outsiders to the field – is still dominated by studies of what were seen as relatively simple societies uncontaminated by outsiders. The literature of colonial anthropology is no longer so subject to this accusation, but it remains the case that only a few of the colonized peoples had the kind of literate, urban, and imperialistic civilization that the ancient Egyptians did. To know what is a relevant point of comparison, one must determine what essential aspects of culture are at stake, and where one may find societies with some similarities in those aspects. It is worth picking one's comparanda carefully.

Equally, ancient historians cannot simply borrow anthropological theory and schemes without criticism. Anthropology is no more monolithic than any other discipline in its analytic frameworks and broad views. The four-part scheme deployed by Will seems to me even more inadequate than he would admit, not simply because it is not complex enough, but because its underlying binary opposition between acceptance and rejection is not very helpful, tending to frame reaction to foreign domination in the outsider's terms. From the point of view of the indigenous population, acceptance and rejection may not be the real choices; even some types of rejection may be types of acceptance.

When the colonized respond in the genre of rational debate – at least as defined in European terms – the hegemony of the colonizing culture may be well on the way to instilling itself in its new subjects; that is why truly counter-hegemonic reactions so frequently seek out alternative modes of expression.[21]

But in a sense this is a diversion from our main point. It is correct, as Will argues, that if we adopt colonialism as a working hypothesis rather than as a description, it opens up a wide range of questions, models, explanations, and characterizations. It is up to us to select critically from among them, put them to the test, and see what their failure or success teaches us. Whatever the limitations, and I have tried to sketch a few, the value of this approach in renovating our range of questions to put to the papyri is enormous. Equally, however, unequal power relations not directly tied to colonialism can offer similarly useful models, and the imagination can be informed by literature as well as by the social sciences.[22]

One example of the discerning and light-handed application of anthropological parallels will be a suitable close to this discussion. At the papyrological congress of 1968, Jean Bingen presented some reflections on a complex and difficult document from the Zenon archive.[23] Panakestor, the estate agent in the Fayum for the finance minister Apollonios, had rented out a substantial parcel of grainland to a group of Egyptian farmers, who were to pay their landlord one-third of the eventual crop. The practice of sharecropping was well known in Egypt and readily understood by the farmers. While the wheat crop was still standing, orders came from Apollonios that the amount of the farmers' payment to him should be established on the basis of an estimation in advance, rather than after the harvest. The precise meaning of this step within this particular context is unclear, but at a minimum it would be analogous to other

Ptolemaic measures to provide the government (in this case, of course, the private landlord) with stable and predictable revenues, thus placing potential risks and rewards of fluctuation in crop size (and perhaps value) on others. Such techniques, including estimation of standing crops, were well-known parts of Greek economic management, but entirely foreign to the Egyptians.

The result of the attempt by Panakestor to put Apollonios' order into effect was that the farmers first replied that they would think about it and answer later. Their answer, a few days later, was to retreat into a temple and refuse to take part in the exercise, preferring to abandon the entire arrangement rather than be party to the process of estimation. Bingen points out that

> flight is a characteristic reaction of an archaic group, in the ethnographic sense of that word, in the face of the intrusion of a more evolved group, and particularly before the intrusion of a group which, being aware of the innovative efficacy of human intervention, disturbs the existing solitary order.

Third-century Egypt, of course, is not a prehistoric peasant culture, nor was the third-century Greek world a modern capitalistic society. But the mechanism of behavior is essentially the same, the simple refusal even to discuss matters, the refusal to play the outsiders' game. Bingen points out that the fact that the peasants flee to the temple rather than simply taking to flight is a measure of the difference between the institutionally well-developed character of Egyptian society and the less institutionalized societies involved in many colonial confrontations of this sort.

The farmers' behavior could be seen as a type of Will's "passive rejection" reaction, the use of withdrawal and strikes; but actually the situation is more complicated. The farmers are very willing to enter into contractual relationships with the outsiders, to help them in the enterprise of agricultural development of new land. But they are willing to do it only in their own way, not with the outsiders' new management techniques. It is certainly possible that Apollonios' attempt to impose advance estimation at this late stage in the agricultural cycle was not a neutral act; the farmers may have been right to see it as a trap they had to avoid. In any case, these farmers are neither simply accepting nor simply rejecting foreign domination; these just are not the categories that appear as choices in their particular situation.

In this case, then, both the similarities of the Egyptian situation to that seen elsewhere and its differences are illuminated by the comparison. Bingen's paper was written for oral presentation (within a time limit) and is interpretive rather than heavily documented. The ethnographic parallels are barely supported by bibliographic citation, let alone explored in detail. But the paper shows something of the gains in understanding that an imagination informed by knowledge of the colonial world can bring to the interpretation of the papyri.

Chapter 7

Continuity and renewal

THE DURABILITY OF PHILOLOGY

There is a certain paradox in the nature of philological study of papyrus texts. On the one hand, we have come to recognize that our texts are humanly constructed, not inescapable facts of nature or something imposed on us by writers of antiquity. In part this is the unavoidable result of the fragmentariness of what has survived; for every complete papyrus, numerous broken ones and still more small fragments survive. But in still larger measure it is the result of the confrontation between editor and papyrus, a process in which reading and interpretation are inextricably intertwined.[1] Peter Parsons has recently put the point succinctly:

> our activities fit with curious aptness into modernist discourse: in the most literal way, our texts are artifacts, our readings are creative. The construction of a text is itself a critical act: decipherment determines supplement, supplements build up context, contexts combine in form, form interrogates readings and supplements, and so circularly; eye and understanding provoke each other.[2]

On the other hand, it is primarily the careful application of philological method that gives us the ability to put hypotheses to the test. In some cases this is precisely a matter of falsifying statements, of showing that a generalization or an explanation cannot be correct. In other cases it may actually be a matter of proving that something is true, of deploying interlocking pieces of evidence to demonstrate a point. It is probably true that the larger the generalization, the more powerful the explanatory statement, the less likely it is that a hypothesis can be shown to be fact. But it remains the case that patient study of the papyri has over the decades produced a large body of exact learning that, though always open to further refinement, is in no danger of being overturned.

It is, moreover, this method that continues to add to the store of evidence for historical investigation. The editing of unpublished texts, the correction of published ones, and even the reediting of the published ones where enough is to be gained, all continue to contribute to both aspects of our paradox. These activities construct and reconstruct texts, and they provide the locus where most of the detailed investigations of the vocabulary and institutions visible in the papyri take place. This activity remains important and, even in the face of all that can be said about its limitations from an historical point of view, is indispensable.[3]

Both sides of the paradox remain critical for historical study, and they are together a large part of the reason why the world of the papyri tends to remain closed to those not trained in papyrological method. The larger aspirations that I shall discuss in the next section collide with the realities of the evidence, both for "insiders" and for "outsiders." The work necessary either to establish a fact or to disprove a hypothesis inescapably requires a prolonged immersion in the texts, both those directly relevant to the question and those providing a larger context without which one may well mistake the significance of something. There is no short cut. For outsiders these are formidable entry fees, and for insiders they leave little time and energy for other work.

And "texts" here means not just the words and sentences, but the dots and brackets, too. Only in looking at these too can the historian get a sense of just how far the footing underneath is solid or spongy. Moreover, the absence of dots may represent nothing more than the editor's unconsciousness of the fragility of the text and of the doubtfulness of the reading. All the more reason that the sense of what is and is not a sound reading needs development in every historian who seeks to work with the papyri – a sense that comes only from reading a lot of texts and from working with the artefacts themselves, from bearing the editor's and critic's burden oneself. It would be pleasant to be able to offer to historians in general the good news that all of that philological baggage and training really is not essential, that the doors have been flung wide open, but this just is not the case. The necessity of sound philological underpinnings to historical work is only part of the explanation of the durability of philology. Its other virtue should be evident from earlier chapters: it remains a fertile source of questions and insights. The best collaboration, as Louis Robert never tired of saying, takes place inside a single brain, and it is above all the well-stocked mind that tends to generate connections previously unnoticed.[4] Sometimes this is simply a matter of drawing links between papyri, and we are far from exhausting the possibilities of these, but I have suggested in particular the enormous untapped potential of connecting the papyri to other bodies of textual material, both in the traditional languages of classical scholarship and in others.[5] The voluminous writers in Greek of the imperial and late antique periods, who are hardly at all read today by students undergoing a classical education, the large corpus of legal writing, the texts in various forms of Egyptian that were drawn up in the same place and at the same time as the Greek papyri, the writings of neighboring ancient cultures like the Jewish legal texts – all these open up large areas where almost everything is still to be done. No particular revolution of method is needed here, only a broadening of the horizons of the textual corpora to be read and thought about.

Indeed, where the reading is broad enough, the full editing of a text may in itself make a substantial historical contribution. An example is to be found in Ludwig Koenen's edition of a Byzantine letter in the Cologne collection, in which the sender very respectfully asks the recipient to copy a book for him on to parchment – whenever it may be convenient for him, naturally.[6] Copyists were generally of low or modest status in monastic communities,[7] and Koenen suggests that the monk addressed and treated so deferentially in this letter may have owed his position to being an anchorite rather than a member of a large monastery. The rich reflections on the standing of a book-copying monk offered in this edition depend on Koenen's exceptionally broad knowledge of the Christian literature of late antiquity and scholarly discussion related to it.

This example makes another important point: philology is particularly critical in work in cultural history, above all at the point where cultural history meets social history, as in this case.

This is most obviously true in literary texts themselves, where the papyri bring us a thousand years closer to the author than anything classical scholarship had available to it before the nineteenth century. Their editing and criticism is preeminently a matter of traditional philological tools.[8] But it is also true in the attentive reading of documentary texts that can tell us something about literary culture.[9]

THE CHALLENGE OF A LARGER CONTEXT

By itself, however, a broadening of the raw materials of classical philology is not enough, and its inadequacy has been increasingly felt by the more thoughtful members of the field. Indeed, it does not even stand up well to the challenge of nineteenth-century *Altertumswissenschaft* at its best, which, as Peter van Minnen has put it, "aimed at encompassing all there was to know about the ancient world, and then to reconstruct ancient culture as a whole – from the bottom up, so to speak."[10] Although this is meant as a nutshell description of what Mommsen and some of his contemporaries were about, it might as well be a capsule summary of the aims of much of what has passed for cutting-edge scholarship in twentieth-century historiography, particularly the French movement associated with the journal *Annales: économies, sociétés, civilisations.*[11] These aims are sometimes expressed in the phrase popularized by Fernand Braudel, "total history."[12]

The work of the *Annales* school has had a powerful attraction for some papyrological historians. James Keenan put it precisely:

First contact with these books had already been for some papyrologists a transforming, enlightening, yet reassuring experience. The reassurance no doubt stemmed from a feeling that Le Roy Ladurie worked with his evidence the way papyrologists could (or did) work with theirs; and from the fact that his work tended to validate the worth of local documentary studies as an historian's enterprise. There is a sense of kinship here because the papyrologist's evidence, like Le Roy Ladurie's, comes almost exclusively from country villages and towns.[13]

Moreover, the kinship of the *Annales* historians with the methods of social anthropology has fitted well with the shape classical scholarship has taken in recent decades under the impact of the work of anthropologically trained French classicists.

Braudel's vision, to which I have already referred in the introduction, was in plan all-embracing, and it would be hard to find any approach or set of questions mentioned in previous chapters that would not find its place in "total history." Indeed, there are many possible sources of useful approaches to the evidence of the papyri left unmentioned in the necessarily selective discussion here, and these too fit well into a Braudelian vision.[14]

The attraction of this enterprise for the papyrological historian is of course not only the natural affinity between styles of work that Keenan describes. It is the sense of opportunity, for Egypt is the one area of the ancient world for which we have anything resembling the evidence needed for total history. Despite all of the caveats sprinkled through this book, despite all of the limitations and fragmentary character of the evidence,[15] the goal is more nearly attainable for Egypt from Alexander to the Arab conquest than for any other part of antiquity. For other times and places, it is not much of an exaggeration to say that the evidence is not so much fragmentary as nonexistent, and that the main reaction of the ancient historian to the work on medieval and early modern Europe by the *Annalistes* can only be envy. If the papyrological historian does not at least make the attempt, one can hardly avoid a sense of lost opportunity.

There are risks in not taking such an opportunity. Probably the most substantial is passive acceptance of a widening gap between the agendas of other disciplines in the humanities and the social sciences and that of papyrology. Both intellectually and professionally there is much at stake. There is a long tradition in papyrology of bewailing its isolation within classical studies, where the supremacy of a classicism bound to an elitist canon has allowed the marginalization of a field that – like epigraphy, similarly treated – offers continuing evidence that the reality of antiquity was very different from this classicism.[16] From the sense that blaming others for this state of affairs is useless (as Bingen puts it) has come a tendency for self-blame and to pointing to real but secondary phenomena like the cost of books.[17] To my mind the structural phenomena described above – the sheer difficulty of both doing papyrology and doing history – are far more central to the increased isolation of papyrology in the postwar period. In any event, the intellectual currents of recent years are in many ways favorable to the materials, questions, and approaches of the history of Egypt under foreign rule, and the opportunity for bringing papyrology out of its ghetto is thereby all the greater.

LIMITS AND PROSPECTS

The most obvious rejoinder to such an appeal for a papyrological version of total history is simply that it is impossible. There is no doubt that it is impossible for any individual. Braudel himself was criticized not only for his intellectual framework, the tripartite wedding-cake structure with the material basis of life at the foot and events as frosting, but for failing to do justice to cultural symbols, ideas, values, religion, and mentalities.[18] The nearest equivalent to Braudel in ancient history was surely Michael Rostovtzeff, particularly the late Rostovtzeff of the *Social and Economic History of the Hellenistic World* (1941), who commanded an extraordinary range of evidence and interests for the whole of the Mediterranean and Near East. Rostovtzeff is open to criticism on many of the same grounds as Braudel, and like Braudel he concerns himself heavily with the material basis of civilization and history. Faced with evidence that exceptional brilliance, erudition, breadth of interests, industry, and longevity are not enough to allow titans like Braudel and Rostovtzeff to write true total histories, and that the philological work required with the papyri greatly increases the scope of the task, what can mere mortals hope for?[19]

The right direction seems to me to be indicated by the fundamental characteristic of history discussed in the introduction, its openness. The "total history" of Braudel is in principle just as impossible as the general philosophical interpretations of history, be they those of Marx or of Toynbee. Even if the evidence were not incurably fragmentary, and even if some prodigy were capable of writing a total history in terms of today's understandings and approaches, new ones would soon

arrive to undo the totalizing character of the work. To return
to an example I used earlier, the greatest of geniuses could not
in 1886 have written a history of the ancient world that took
into account the methods of modern demography. Moreover,
it is a fundamental characteristic of papyrology, as of epigraphy,
to be constantly contributing new evidence. The discipline is
one of "permanent revision," in Jean Bingen's phrase.[20] The
total history of today would be obsolete tomorrow, then, for
reasons both of evidence and approach.

Even the total history as of today momentarily hypothesized
above, however – a history limited to what can be known today
– is an impossibility, for the unbounded diversity of useful
approaches is a fact not merely of the passage of time but of
human nature. Aptitude for particular paths to understanding
the past is deeply rooted in individual personality and cast of
mind. Scholars are fond of noticing the ways, obvious or
evident, in which their colleagues' work is connected to the rest
of their lives, but they do not necessarily draw any inference
from them. People are not unidimensional, of course, and most
scholars have multiple strengths as well. But they – we – have
our limits as well. It is pointless to blame a book or its author
for being interested in some things and not others; one might
as well criticize the author for not being oneself. It is, of course,
very interesting to point out such limitations, but what is really
interesting is not what is lacking but what is present.

The conclusion of this train of thought is to my mind cheerful
rather than gloomy. It sees the relationship of actual history to
total history as that of an approach to a goal that cannot be
reached, and it sees actual history as the enterprise of a complex
community rather than of an individual. Although like most
complex systems this one looks remarkably disorderly and
confusing from any particular vantage point at any given
moment, it offers rich diversity and a combination of dynamism
and stability. For the individual, it offers a host of specific
niches, each of them different. No two historians have the same
gifts to bring to the task, and no two will use them to the same
ends. There is room enough, in the work of using the papyri to
write the history of the ancient world, for a wide range of
interests, from a purely internal and purely philological concentration on creating, improving, and explicating the texts before

us to a variety of approaches bringing other bodies of material and the insights of other disciplines to bear on the papyri.[21] This catholicity should not, however, obscure the fundamental need of papyrology to enter more fully into the methods and insights of other fields and to apply them to our material. The risks of doing so are considerable, for experimental forays are at least as likely to fail to achieve their ostensible objectives as to succeed in doing so. But even the failures are likely to be enlightening, and in reality most "failures" may be so only by inappropriate standards. Comparative history, for example, serves as much to define the contrasts between societies as to bring out their structural similarities, and the colonial models evoked by Edouard Will in the article discussed in chapter 6 seem to me a microcosm of this process. He offered them with at least some sense that they would prove to resemble conditions in Ptolemaic Egypt, but this need not be the case for one to feel that something has been learned about Egypt in the process.

The practical problems of mastering a difficult technical discipline and simultaneously engaging the broader perspectives needed to write history as it is written today remain daunting. To them I see three principal answers. The first is that one need not master all disciplines and all approaches to make a contribution of value. The would-be historian working with papyri can choose a particular area congenial to his or her aptitudes and interests, reading in some relevant broader intellectual domain, and gradually construct an approach and expertise from which others can learn. In time it may be possible to branch out from this secure base. The second is collaboration with other scholars. This need not, and indeed should not, take the simplistic form of papyrologist as drudge working with historian as thinker, nor will one person play the same role at all times.[22] But complementary strengths, methods, and interests can lead to work that neither collaborator could have done separately. The papyri offer material of interest to scholars in many fields, and we should not imagine that the collaboration is of benefit only to the papyrological member of a partnership or team.

The third answer is not to abandon the hope of attracting historians whose training is outside papyrology to the work of using the papyri for the writing of history. Despite all of the technical hurdles, it is not impossible. An important proof is at hand in Dennis Kehoe's recent book on management of and investment in agricultural estates in Roman Egypt, which springs from a desire to test against the evidence of the papyri a hypothesis about the behavior of landowners formed in Kehoe's study of other evidence for various parts of the Roman empire, particularly his examination of Pliny's letters, but also study of inscriptions from North Africa and the legal codes.[23] The book thus brings into the discussion an externally derived model. The utility of this model seems to me more its ability to throw into relief the complexity of the situation reflected in our evidence than its full congruence with that situation. But that is no mean accomplishment, and the book is a symbol of what can be done by an historian willing to invest time in treating the papyri as simply another body of evidence to be explored.

The stakes in such bridge-building, be it within an individual's work or by collaboration, are large, for they involve the future of ancient studies as an intellectual field and as a viable part of the academic world. In his presidential address to the American Philological Association in 1992, Erich Gruen sounded a clear call to classical studies to seize the extraordinary opportunity that the growth of interest in cultural identity and the interaction of cultures offers for, as he put it, "Few societies have ever been more multicultural than those clustered about the Mediterranean."[24] Within the world of the ancient Mediterranean, no society offers the array of evidence for the workings of cultural interaction in the lives of a wide spectrum of individuals that the Egypt of the papyri does; and to the extent that we come to be able to understand other parts of the ancient world as we can Egypt, it will be by discoveries of papyrus-like texts. Historians working with papyri thus have an opening to many of the liveliest areas of contemporary thought, even if taking advantage of it will make exceptional demands on their ability to maintain a high standard of technical competence in traditional philological disciplines while expanding their intellectual horizons.

Notes

PREFACE

1 This aspect of the papyri will not receive much attention in this book. Cf. P. Parsons (1980) II (where the phrase occurs) for some good examples from private letters. See section X of the General Bibliography for articles in which more, particularly for the Roman period, can be found.
2 There are some good exceptions, notably Beaucamp (1990, 1992) and Kehoe (1992).
3 Exceptions come mostly in the form of brief remarks embedded in substantive investigations. A short general discussion of some aspects (notably the analytic character of the documentation) can be found in W. Peremans and E. van 't Dack (1979). Despite its title, Claire Préaux's article "Papyrologie et sociologie" (C. Préaux 1959) has hardly any methodological content.
4 Funding came from the National Endowment for the Humanities, Interpretive Research Program. I am grateful to the Endowment for its support and to my co-organizer Dirk Obbink for his help.

INTRODUCTION: HISTORY AND PAPYRI

1 Most systematically discussed in S. D. Goitein (1967–88). An attractive sense of the possibilities of the Geniza, which often exceed those of the papyri, can be found in A. Ghosh (1992).
2 E.g., W. Peremans and E. van 't Dack (1979).
3 Cf. B. Frier (1989). Since he wrote, however, the appearance of Beaucamp (1992) and Kehoe (1992) have shown that the barriers can be overcome.
4 E.g., M. I. Finley (1973), who consistently avoids a serious engagement with the Egyptian evidence, or E. Paglagean (1977).
5 It is convincingly refuted for the economy by D. Rathbone (1989).
6 R. Merton (1967) 39.
7 A. Gurevich (1992) 33. Gurevich believes that "It is hard to imagine a scholar without a theory, even if only an implicit one."

8   See the interesting and nuanced account of I. Morris (1994).
9   A. Danto (1985) 1–16; quotations from pp. 14 and 16.
10 Cf. P. Burke (1992) 20.
11 Cf. L. Stone (1985/94) 32, arguing that material and cultural factors interact rather than being related hierarchically (with material factors the more basic), in the manner of Braudel's approach. Cf. below, chapter 7, p. 112, for further discussion of the *Annales* approaches.
12 For a discussion of this concept, see R.K. Merton (1967) 39–72 (the quote is from p. 39).
13 P. Burke (1992) chapters 3 and 4.
14 Cf. A. Danto (1985) 111–15.
15 M. Bloch (1953) 145–6.
16 For a good example see B.D. Palmer (1990), a sweeping attack on the poststructuralist movement couched in remarkably vehement terms.
17 For a recent general defense of this position see J. Appleby, L. Hunt, and M. Jacob (1994); despite the breathless and sometimes intellectually shallow account they give, the book is very levelheaded in its conclusions. Interesting also is B. Stock (1990), esp. 76 ff. For a more philosophically compelling approach to the possibilities of objective knowledge and an excellent demolition of *ad hominem* skepticism, see A. Danto (1985), ch. 6 (unknown to Appleby *et al.*).
18 See the good discussion of P. Carrard (1992) 224–5; also R. Martin (1989), esp. 105–10.
19 R. Martin (1989) is a good example.
20 This tendency can be seen clearly in the essays in P. Burke (1991), each taking a particular type of "new history" to expound.
21 This argument owes a good deal to A. Danto (1985).
22 See R.S. Bagnall and B. Frier (1994).
23 F. Braudel (1980) 131; cf. his remarks on p. 34.
24 As in the curiously archaic notion that anthropology is distinguished from history by its interest in processes rather than events: J. and J. Comaroff (1992) 37. This work is also notable for starting with a whole series of statements about what their historical anthropology is not (p. 20).
25 E. Le Roy Ladurie (1981) 11.
26 In J. Le Goff and P. Nora (1985) 18. To be fair, Furet admits that his statement is untrue if the sources simply do not exist, which is often the case with antiquity.

1   THE CULTURE OF PAPYRUS

1   E. G. Turner (1968, 1980²) is the standard work in English. An Italian manual with extensive bibliography is O. Montevecchi (1973, 1988²). A shorter but well-organized manual by H.-A.

Rupprecht (1994) is very useful. Additional introductory works are listed in the General Bibliography.

2 This is at least true of traditional Egyptian ink, although the Greeks may have introduced the use of metallic elements into it: cf. W. Clarysse (1993) 189.

3 A roster of these finds can be found in H. M. Cotton, W. E. H. Cockle, and F. G. B. Millar (1995).

4 A. Grohmann (1963) introduction.

5 See among the editions *P.Ness.*, *P.Mur.*, *P.Babatha*, *P.Dura*, *O.Bu Njem*, *Doc.Masada*; for the upper Euphrates, D. Feissel and J. Gascou (1989); for Petra, provisionally G. L. Peterman (1993).

6 M. Gigante (1979); A. K. Bowman and J. D. Thomas (1994); A. K. Bowman (1994).

7 See G. Woolf (1994) for a description of the pre-Roman finds of writing in various types of media from western Europe.

8 Some of the earlier rolls from Herculaneum seem to have been written at Athens.

9 See D. Rathbone (1989).

10 See still W. V. Harris (1989) 206 n. 157 for an example.

11 See especially *P.Babatha*, intro.; H. Cotton (1994); D. Feissel and J. Gascou (1989); information from J. Frösén about the Petra papyri. The inscriptions on stone naturally have their own set of practices, as different from the papyri as the contents.

12 For papyrus manufacture see N. Lewis (1974), for prices 129–34, and (1989), for prices 40–1. T. C. Skeat (1982), places the cost somewhat lower, but still a couple of days' wages.

13 A. K. Bowman and J. D. Thomas (1994) for Vindolanda; for Kellis, see J. L. Sharpe (1992).

14 See generally on this theme the essays in A. K. Bowman and G. Woolf (1994).

15 Both copies survive in a certain number of cases.

16 The successive religious entities of Egypt, mainly the Egyptian temples and later the Christian church, have some characteristics of government and some of large private households in their production of documents.

17 For example, these categories (including the affairs of religious establishments) amount to some 87 percent of the texts in *SB* VI; almost all of the rest are private letters. As this series excludes literary and subliterary texts, the figure must be adjusted for these categories. There is no full census of either documents or literary texts, even for published papyri, but I would estimate the literary papyri amount to about 10 percent of the total. As literary papyri tend to be published more quickly than documents, that figure is no doubt an overestimate for those found. Overall, I suppose that the categories mentioned here might well include something over 80 percent of all Greek papyri.

18 See preliminarily the insightful article of P. J. Parsons (1980).

19 See R. Cribiore, forthcoming.

20 See generally W. V. Harris (1989). For the breadth of the popu-
    lation educated, cf. A. K. Bowman (1994).
21 See A. K. Bowman (1994).

2 ANCIENT AND MODERN CHOICES IN DOCUMENTATION

1   See D. M. Lewis (1994) for the interplay of languages and scripts
    in the Persian administration.
2   W. Clarysse (1985) 62–4 (quotation from p. 64), summarizing J.
    Yoyotte (1969).
3   See P. Tebt. Tait for some papyrus examples of the Ptolemaic and
    Roman periods.
4   See J. D. Ray (1994) for a general discussion with many good
    remarks about the formalized character of all of these Egyptian
    scripts.
5   See D. J. Thompson (1994) for the official use of Demotic in the
    fourth and third centuries.
6   See R. S. Bagnall (1993a) 236–8 for this process.
7   On the temples, see R. S. Bagnall (1993a) 236–8 and 261–8; for
    Roman documentary practice, N. Lewis (1993), about whose
    conclusions I have reservations.
8   D. J. Thompson (1988), using Egyptological evidence very ex-
    tensively in reconstructing the life of Ptolemaic Memphis.
9   P. W. Pestman (1978).
10 W. Clarysse (1985).
11 There are of course exceptions; cf. W. Clarysse (1985) 65.
12 P. W. Pestman (1992).
13 Letters are common from the fourth century on, however, even
    apparently in Nubia: see L. Török (1988). It might be noted that
    there are sixth-century Coptic legal documents clearly modelled on
    Greek exemplars: see L. Papini (1983).
14 Including its gnostic wing and Manicheism, with which Christianity
    had such a close and difficult relationship.
15 More numerous, of course, are the documentary texts from the Bay
    of Naples and from Vindolanda mentioned earlier.
16 J. D. Ray (1994) 51.
17 Apart from a handful of texts included here but actually of rather
    different types.
18 See J. G. Keenan (1993).
19 See P. Petaus, introd.; H. C. Youtie (1966a).
20 See, e.g., P. Panop. Beatty.
21 Such existed in modern times. See V. B. Schuman (1972). This is,
    however, perhaps a pattern more of Egyptian than of Greek letter-
    writing; for significant differences between the two cf. J. D. Ray
    (1994) 60. P. J. Parsons (1980) 7–8 and 16 n. 63, finds no evidence
    that there were such public letter-writers in Roman Egypt.

22 See generally K. Preisendanz (1933), now very out of date but invaluable for the earlier period.
23 For a useful discussion see D. J. Thompson (1994), who notes that cartonnage is an innovation of the Ptolemaic period. Despite the difficulties noted here she is inclined to see the early Ptolemaic finds as good evidence for an increase in the overall amount of writing and their patterns as meaningful, cf. esp. p. 71. I remain much less certain.
24 Cf. P. van Minnen (1994). The situation is similar with the unpublished Coptic ostraka from excavations at Deir el-Bahri and the Monastery of Epiphanius, now in the collection of Columbia University, for most of which precise provenances are recorded.
25 *P.Brux.* 1–19.
26 *P.Thmouis* I, *P.Bub.* I.
27 See, e.g., *O.Claud.* I, *O.Douch* I-III, *P.Quseir,* and G. Wagner (1987).
28 This section is based on R. S. Bagnall (1988).
29 It is true, as Dirk Obbink points out to me, that sometimes the physical disposition of the restoration (e.g., the number of letters that must be on a particular line because of the rules of syllabication) may provide useful information, especially about space remaining.

3 PARTICULAR AND GENERAL

1 On this controversy see A. Martin (1994) and below, p. 40.
2 R. Rémondon (1964), discussing *UPZ* I 148.
3 The editors note, however, that the handwriting would to their eyes belong a bit later, citing a similar hand dated to 226/7.
4 P. van Minnen (1986a).
5 The specific designation of an individual in the list as a councillor, however, makes it unlikely that this was a list entirely of councillors. The relatively large number of names concentrated in a small part of the alphabet is also incompatible with supposing this list to represent only the council, the membership of which is unlikely to have been larger than 100. It is more probable that this is a list of men with membership in the defined body of metropolitan citizens.
6 A similar phenomenon occurs again after the Arab conquest, when lists of the Arabic equivalents of Greek and Coptic names are found; an example is British Library MS. Or. 1325 (information from Leslie MacCoull).
7 The editors offer no examples of lists which do include Aurelius. Instances without it from the third and fourth centuries are fairly common; one from early in the third century (but after the Antonine Constitution) is the (still unpublished) register from Philadelphia in the Yale collection, inv. 296.
8 *P.Cair.Masp.* II 67126.
9 J. G. Keenan (1992).
10 See the discussion of G. Levi in P. Burke (1991) 93–110.
11 P. J. Parsons (1980) 8 with 16–17 n. 64.

12 H. C. Youtie (1970).
13 There has been a controversy within papyrology about the applic-
    ability of the term 'archive' to clusters of texts not demonstrably
    collected and classified intentionally in antiquity. For a judicious
    summary see A. Martin (1994). His distinction between archive and
    dossier, however, lightly modified from P. W. Pestman and J.
    Modrzejewski, encounters the terminological difficulty that (at
    least to my ears) 'dossier' suggests planned classification almost as
    much as 'archive' does and thus fails to offer the needed contrast.
    For the moment, I have allowed myself the commonplace latitude
    of papyrological usage, albeit with some uneasiness. A list of
    archives, constructed on latitudinarian principles, can be found in
    Montevecchi (1988²) 248–61, 575–8.
14 See A. E. Hanson (1989) for a description of the process in this
    case.
15 *P.Mich.* X 582.
16 J. G. Keenan (1980).
17 But working earlier; D. S. Crawford died in 1952 and the volume
    (*P.Michael.*) was seen through press by Eric Turner.
18 *P.Mich.* II 121, 123; V 238.
19 D. W. Hobson (1984a).
20 This is not to say that even the most atypical are without interest
    to the historian, naturally, particularly in microhistorical ap-
    proaches; cf. p. 38.
21 D. W. Hobson (1983).
22 Apart from the one discussed here, it should be noted that the
    Zenon archive has been the subject of several books, from M. I.
    Rostovtzeff's classic *A Large Estate in Egypt in the Third Century* BC
    (1922) to C. Orrieux (1983) and (1985). D. J. Thompson (1988),
    though wide-ranging in its documentation, is in large part an
    extended study of the archive of the Memphis Sarapieion.
23 The following discussion is based on my review of the book in R.
    S. Bagnall (1993b).
24 This point is not demonstrated as convincingly as others, in my
    view.
25 It has now been shown by W. Clarysse and C. Gallazzi (1993) that
    Laches is only an employee of the family, not the ancestor.
26 Cited above, n. 22.
27 W. Clarysse (1992).
28 The settler in question, Maron son of Euphranor, "Libyan" born
    in Egypt, has (as Clarysse notes, *P.Petr.*² I 1, note to line 38) a name
    popular in Egypt because it could be used as a Greek "equivalent"
    to the Egyptian name Marres. Some Egyptian influence may also
    be visible here.
29 D. W. Hobson (1984b).
30 It strikes me, in fact, as very questionable. Briefly: (1) Wheat taxes
    were based on arable land, and a village with a small and fluctuating
    base of such land should have had a small and adjustable wheat-tax
    burden. (2) A prosperous village could always buy wheat with its

cash income to meet any wheat-tax burdens that did exist. (3) The hypothesis takes no account of other changes in the economic environment, notably the striking decline of temples throughout Egypt in the second and third centuries.

31 *O.Elkab* publishes the Roman ostraka by place of finding. Although *O.Claud.* I does not give much attention to these connections, future publications will do so, as a paper given by Jean Bingen at the British Museum in December, 1993, indicates. For Karanis, see P. van Minnen (1994).

32 G. Husson (1979).

33 G. Husson (1983).

34 See now also the important article of E. Wipszycka (1994) 1–44.

35 J. Quaegebeur (1989).

4 TIME AND PLACE

1 R. S. Bagnall and K. A. Worp (1978), chapter 4.

2 *P.Oxy.* LVIII, pp. 51–7.

3 D. Hagedorn (1985), esp. 187–92.

4 It is possible, but so far not demonstrated, that some were even private functionaries.

5 Hagedorn suggests that the official of AD 63 might be a staff officer of the prefect's administration, hence normally invisible, and a forerunner of the later procuratorial appointment.

6 Cf. *P.Col.* VIII 211, another example of the lower-level local Augustan official.

7 J. D. Thomas (1975).

8 On which the classic discussion is P. J. Parsons (1967). Thomas's conclusion also allows him to redate substantially (and, I believe, convincingly) one of the major texts at stake in the controversy, *P.Lond.* III 1157.

9 M. Drew-Bear (1988).

10 Drew-Bear draws heavily on the work of Louis Robert, who frequently discussed these inscriptions in detail.

11 N. Lewis (1981).

12 Cf. L. S. B. MacCoull (1992) for an argument that for the late Roman period Egypt must be seen *primarily* in its connection to the wider world.

13 A good general treatment of the subject may be found in J. G. Keenan (1975). J. Beaucamp (1990, 1992) is very much devoted to this problem, with respect to the legislation concerning women; see my review in Bagnall (1995).

14 J.-M. Carrié (1993). Only the first of several topics discussed by Carrié in this article can be treated here, and the argument has been simplified in certain respects.

15 For a general treatment, see J. A. Sheridan (1995).

16 A. K. Bowman and D. Rathbone (1992).

17 *Historiae* 1.11: "a province difficult of access, prolific of grain,

disturbed and divided by religious and other passions, knowing nothing of laws and ignorant of magistrates."

18 N. Lewis (1970); see also his follow-up remarks fifteen years later: N. Lewis (1984).
19 A. K. Bowman and D. Rathbone (1992) 124–5.
20 D. W. Hobson (1988) 355.
21 See R. S. Bagnall (1993a) 48–54.
22 L. S. B. MacCoull (1992).
23 These comments are based mainly on extended visits to the Fayum in September, 1989 and April, 1993.
24 These are respectively D. W. Hobson (1989), J. G. Keenan (1989), R. S. Bagnall (1989), and B. W. Frier (1989).
25 B. W. Frier (1989) 225 n. 27.
26 See P. C. Maddern (1992), which is very strong on the "quintessentially hierarchical" nature of the "moral order of violence" (p. 228).
27 J. G. Keenan (1985).
28 The answer seems almost certainly to be that the main meat eaten in antiquity was pork – a clear case in which a radical change has overtaken Egypt since the Arab conquest.

5 QUANTIFICATION

1 Cf., e.g., J. Appleby, L. Hunt, and M. Jacob (1994) 87.
2 A couple of random instances: M. I. Finley (1974) 23–4; A. H. M. Jones (1964) viii.
3 See particularly two books by R. Duncan-Jones (1974, 1982²) and (1990), both using papyri but in a secondary role, the inscriptions and authors being the main sources used.
4 In a paper at the 1993 Byzantine Studies Conference, Angeliki Laïou called attention to the pitfalls inherent in constructing the data for some such inquiries. This tends to be less of a difficulty with the papyri, but it needs to be borne in mind, and it is very germane to the questions at stake in the concluding section of this chapter (pp. 85–9).
5 P. van Minnen and K. A. Worp (1993) 182.
6 M. Bloch (1953) 120.
7 This section is based on and partly drawn from R. S. Bagnall (1992), where full documentation and discussion of various aspects not treated here are provided.
8 P. J. Sijpesteijn and K. A. Worp (1978).
9 A. K. Bowman (1985).
10 This pattern can already be seen in the Florentine Catasto of 1427; see D. Herlihy and C. Klapisch-Zuber (1985) 93–105.
11 P. van Minnen (1986b).
12 Equally, van Minnen's hypothesis deals with the imprecision problem; export duties would naturally be levied on broad classes of garments.

13 See R. S. Bagnall and B. W. Frier (1994) 102–03.
14 These are studied in detail for their demographic information in R. S. Bagnall and B. W. Frier (1994), on which what follows is based. I cannot here discuss the problems inherent in the other classes of evidence sometimes deployed for demographic purposes, particularly funerary inscriptions; the reader is referred to our book and to T. G. Parkin (1992).
15 Supposing 17 censuses and about a million households reporting in each.
16 R. S. Bagnall and B. W. Frier (1994) 82 with figure 4.2; the raw data have been put through a smoothing process (using moving averages) to damp out the fluctuations.
17 A very similar situation is found, once again, in the Florentine Catasto, where D. Herlihy and C. Klapisch-Zuber (1985) 131–44 show that despite the many sources of error in the data that may have exaggerated the sex ratio, not all of the excess male population found in the data can be attributed to such evidentiary problems; there must be underlying social causes for much of it.
18 See the appendix on statistical methods in R. S. Bagnall and B. W. Frier (1994) 330–33 for a brief exposition.
19 This discussion continues to be lively; I plan to give an account of it on another occasion.
20 R. S. Bagnall (1982).
21 R. W. Bulliet (1979).
22 Some assumptions had to be made about the average age of these groups and the length of generations, of course; these are not germane to the methodological points at stake here.
23 Broadly speaking, the analysis suggests that Christians formed the majority sometime in the second half of the fourth century.
24 R. S. Bagnall (1987).
25 She conceded several points about the evidence. Her concluding paragraph (E. Wipszycka [1988] 165) appears to respond to my criticism of her final point, but she does not seem to have understood it and her comment is not relevant.
26 It should be pointed out that the date of the register that I originally took to be from 388 is now certain to be later, perhaps second half of the fifth century. On the other side of the ledger, the archive of Papnouthis and Dorotheos in P.Oxy. XLVIII has added some material from the poorly documented second half of the fourth century.
27 I am grateful to Professor Stark for sending me a copy of part of his forthcoming book on this subject.

6 ASKING QUESTIONS

1 B. W. Frier (1989) 217.
2 J. Gascou (1976).
3 Particularly A. Cameron (1973) and (1976), preliminary articles for which Gascou had seen.

4 J. Gascou (1976) 186.
5 R. Katzoff (1985).
6 R. Katzoff (1985) 231–2.
7 R. Katzoff (1985) 241–2.
8 Katzoff rightly sets aside Seidl's invocation of Codex Justinianus 5.15.1, which cannot be shown to have any connection with Egypt.
9 Wipszycka points to other causes as well, notably a change in mentality which increasingly adopted a high view of clerical privileges and duties, reserving these for a smaller number of clergy.
10 D. W. Hobson (1989).
11 S. B. Pomeroy (1986) 147–62: itself a pure example of intensive internal analysis of the papyrological data.
12 B. W. Frier (1989) 222.
13 Cf. M. W. Dickie (1993) 9–26.
14 Indeed, hypotheses generally are not proved; they are tested, and either they are disproved or they survive and await further testing or modification.
15 Pomeroy lists *P.Erl.* 93 as AD 7–8, but it is second or third century (*BL* 8.121). She also lists *SB* X 10529, but a rereading has eliminated the name (*BL* 7.221).
16 E. Will (1985).
17 Particularly M. I. Rostovtzeff (1941) and C. Préaux (1939).
18 A striking parallel exists in the development of wage labor in South Africa, also to meet tax burdens: see J. and J. Comaroff (1992) 162–3 etc.
19 Again well paralleled in South Africa, cf. J. and J. Comaroff (1992) 128 etc.
20 Some evidence from the Roman period seems to me to indicate reasonably quick turnaround time, much faster than modern courts offer; cf. R. S. Bagnall (1993a) 169–70.
21 J. and J. Comaroff (1992) 257. See also the discussion of peasant reactions in J. C. Scott (1985), from which it is clear that much of what is classified by the typology Will invokes as "passive acceptance" is actually a form of resistance.
22 I discuss this subject in more detail in a forthcoming article.
23 J. Bingen (1970).

7   CONTINUITY AND RENEWAL

1 See the classic descriptions of H. C. Youtie (1963), (1966b), (1974). A good sense of the same process at work in literary texts can be had in E. G. Turner (1973).
2 P. J. Parsons (1994) 122.
3 Cf. the remarks of B. W. Frier (1989) and J. Bingen (1994). Bingen rejects the adjective "antiquarian" in reference to this work, Frier accepts it but rejects any pejorative sense.
4 Robert's writings about epigraphical method are perhaps more

useful to the papyrologist interested in philological method than anything about the papyri themselves. They are largely scattered; most are indexed in the *Index du Bulletin épigraphique de J. et L. Robert, 1938–1965* III (Paris 1975) 1–6. Cf. also the *Index . . . 1968–1973* 416 s.v. méthode for some additions. The most systematic of his treatments is L. Robert (1961).

5   The benefits flow both ways. For an example of the utility of the papyri in looking at philosophical works of late antiquity, see L. S. B. MacCoull forthcoming.

6   L. Koenen (1975).

7   Cf. the discussion of R. Lane Fox in A. K. Bowman and G. Woolf (1994) 130–31.

8   E. G. Turner (1968) 97–126 gives a good survey of the impact of the papyri on literary studies, including on textual criticism.

9   Cf. above, chapter 3, p. 39, for Youtie's identification of a tax clerk who knew Callimachus.

10   P. van Minnen (1993) 9.

11   It should be remembered, of course, that many of the same currents of thought visible in the *Annales* movement were equally and independently present in other countries early in this century and even earlier; cf. P. Burke (1990), chapters 1 and 5.

12   See P. Burke (1990) 114 on this term. J. G. Keenan (1991) speaks of this as a tendency to "totalize," but that term has acquired meanings in contemporary discourse that make it of doubtful use here.

13   J. G. Keenan (1991) 160. Le Roy Ladurie has actually been criticized for failings we would call philological, cf. P. Burke (1990) 82–3. Keenan's last point seems to me not entirely accurate; places like Oxyrhynchos and Hermopolis were considerably more than "country towns."

14   Most prominently one might mention contemporary currents in literary criticism, including the New Historicism pointed to by P. van Minnen (1993) 10 as an example of a fruitful avenue.

15   Pointed to by P. van Minnen (1993) 9 as the "major drawback" of the approach of *Altertumswissenschaft.*

16   See most recently P. van Minnen (1993) and J. Bingen (1994).

17   There is no doubt, to be sure, that papyrologists share with every other field of academic endeavor a tendency to write for excessively specialized audiences too much of the time. But that is an unremarkable and probably unavoidable byproduct of the professionalization of scholarship, the solution to which certainly does not lie in eliminating technical scholarship.

18   See P. Burke (1990) 38–42, 51–3.

19   An instructive contrast is offered by Louis Robert, himself easily describable in the same words, but who consistently steered himself away from large-scale synthetic history and never wrote the promised works from which one might most have expected such history. Some of his articles might well be oxymoronically described as total microhistory, and Robert had a Braudelian interest in the historical

geography and the material basis of life. But he also took considerable interest in cultural and symbolic aspects.
20 J. Bingen (1977) 36.
21 Cf. J. Bingen (1994) 47, quoting his own remark (1977) that there
are as many papyrologies as papyrologists, and warning against the
creation of a hierarchy of fields within the discipline.
22 In my own collaborative work I have at times been the more
historical, at times the more philological partner, and I have found
both rewarding.
23 D. P. Kehoe (1992). See my review article in R. S. Bagnall (1993)
from which some of the comments here are drawn.
24 E. S. Gruen (1993) 2.

Works cited in the text and notes

Note: *BASP* = *Bulletin of the American Society of Papyrologists*; *CP* = *Classical Philology*; *GRBS* = *Greek, Roman and Byzantine Studies*; *JRS* = *Journal of Roman Studies*; *ZPE* = *Zeitschrift für Papyrologie und Epigraphik*. Other journal titles are given in full.

Appleby, J., Hunt, L., and Jacob, M. (1994). *Telling the Truth About History* (New York).

Bagnall, R. S. (1982). "Religious conversion and onomastic change in early Byzantine Egypt," *BASP* 19: 105–24.

—— (1987). "Conversion and onomastics: a reply," *ZPE* 69: 243–50.

—— (1988). "Restoring the text of documents," *Text. Transactions of the Society for Textual Scholarship* 4: 109–19.

—— (1989). "Official and private violence in Roman Egypt," *BASP* 26: 201–16.

—— (1992). "Landholding in late Roman Egypt: the distribution of wealth," *JRS* 82: 128–49.

—— (1993a). *Egypt in Late Antiquity* (Princeton).

—— (1993b). Review of Rathbone (1991), *JRS* 83: 254–6.

—— (1993c). "Managing estates in Roman Egypt: a review article," *BASP* 30: 127–35.

—— (1995). "Women, law, and social realities in late antiquity: a review article," *BASP* 32.

Bagnall, R. S., and Frier, B. W. (1994). *The Demography of Roman Egypt* (Cambridge).

Bagnall, R. S., and Worp, K. A. (1978). *Chronological Systems of Byzantine Egypt* (Stud. Amst. 8, Zutphen).

Beaucamp, J. (1990, 1992). *Le statut de la femme à Byzance (4e-7e siècle)* (Travaux et Mémoires du Centre de Recherche d'Histoire et Civilisation de Byzance, Collège de France, Monographies; Paris). I, *Le droit impérial* (Monographies 5, 1990); II, *Les pratiques sociales* (Monographies 6, 1992).

Bingen, J. (1970). "Grecs et Égyptiens d'après *PSI* 502," *Proceedings of the Twelfth International Congress of Papyrology* (Toronto) 35–40.

—— (1977). "La papyrologie grecque et latine: problèmes de fond et problèmes d'organisation," *Aspects des études classiques*, ed. J. Bingen and G. Cambier (Brussels) 33–44.

—— (1994). "D'avant-hier à demain," *Proceedings of the 20th International Congress of Papyrologists* (Copenhagen) 42–47.

Bloch, M. (1953). *The Historian's Craft* (New York).

Bowman, A. K. (1985). "Landholding in the Hermopolite nome in the fourth century AD," *JRS* 75: 137–63.

—— (1994). "The Roman imperial army: letters and literacy on the northern frontier," in Bowman and Woolf (1994) 109–25.

Bowman, A. K., and Rathbone, D. (1992). "Cities and administration in Roman Egypt," *JRS* 82: 107–27.

Bowman, A. K., and Thomas, J. D. (1994). *The Vindolanda Writing Tablets (Tabulae Vindolandenses* II) (London).

Bowman, A. K., and Woolf, G., eds. (1994). *Literacy and Power in the Ancient World* (Cambridge).

Braudel, F. (1980). *On History* (Chicago).

Bulliet, R. W. (1979). *Conversion to Islam in the Medieval Period* (Cambridge, Mass.).

Burke, P. (1990). *The French Historical Revolution. The Annales School, 1929–89* (Cambridge/Oxford).

—— (1991). *New Perspectives on Historical Writing* (Cambridge/Oxford).

—— (1992). *History and Social Theory* (Cambridge/Oxford).

Cameron, A. (1973). *Porphyrius the Charioteer* (Oxford).

—— (1976). *Circus Factions* (Oxford).

Carrard, P. (1992). *Poetics of the New History: French Historical Discourse from Braudel to Chartier* (Baltimore).

Carrié, J.-M. (1993). "Observations sur la fiscalité du IVᵉ siècle pour servir à l'histoire monétaire," *L'"inflazione" nel quarto secolo d.C. Atti dell'incontro di studio Roma 1988* (Istituto Italiano di Numismatica, Studi e Materiali 3, Rome) 115–54.

Clarysse, W. (1985). "Greeks and Egyptians in the Ptolemaic army and administration," *Aegyptus* 65: 57–66.

—— (1992). "Some Greeks in Egypt," *Life in a Multi-cultural Society: Egypt from Cambyses to Constantine and Beyond*, ed. Janet H. Johnson (SAOC 51, Chicago) 51–56.

—— (1993). "Egyptian scribes writing Greek," *Chronique d'Égypte* 68: 189.

—— and Gallazzi, C. (1993). "Archivio dei discendenti di Laches o dei discendenti di Patron?" *Ancient Society* 24: 63–8.

Comaroff, J. and J. (1992). *Ethnography and the Historical Imagination* (Boulder, Colorado).

Cotton, H. (1994). "A cancelled marriage contract from the Judaean desert," *JRS* 84: 64–86

Cotton, H. M., Cockle, W. E. H., and Millar, F. G. B. (1995). "The papyrology of the Roman Near East: a survey," *JRS* 85.

Cribiore, R. (forthcoming). *Writing, Teachers and Students in Graeco-Roman Egypt* (Atlanta).

Danto, A. (1985). *Narration and Knowledge* (New York).

Dickie, M. W. (1993). "Malice, envy and inquisitiveness in Catullus 5 and 7," *Papers of the Leeds International Latin Seminar* 7: 9–26.

Drew-Bear, M. (1988). "Les athlètes d'Hermoupolis Magna et leur ville au 3ᵉ siècle," *Proceedings of the XVIII International Congress of Papyrology* (Athens): II 229–35.

Duncan-Jones, R. (1974, 1982²). *The Economy of the Roman Empire: Quantitative Studies* (Cambridge).

—— (1990). *Structure and Scale in the Roman Economy* (Cambridge).

Feissel, D. and Gascou, J. (1989). "Documents d'archives romains inédits du moyen Euphrate (IIIᵉ siècle après J.-C.)," *Comptes Rendus de l'Académie des Inscriptions et Belles-Lettres* (1989) 535–61.

Finley, M. I. (1973). *The Ancient Economy* (Berkeley).

Frier, B. W. (1989). "A new papyrology?" *BASP* 26: 217–26.

Gascou, J. (1976). "Les institutions de l'hippodrome en Égypte byzantine," *Bulletin de l'Institut Français d'Archéologie Orientale* 76: 185–212.

Ghosh, A. (1992). *In an Antique Land* (London).

Gigante, M. (1979). *Catalogo dei Papiri Ercolanesi* (Naples).

Goitein, S. D. (1967–88). *A Mediterranean Society*, 5 vols. (Berkeley).

Grohmann, A. (1963). *Arabic Papyri from Hirbet el-Mird* (Louvain).

Gruen, E. S. (1993). "Cultural fictions and cultural identity," *Transactions of the American Philological Association* 123: 1–14.

Gurevich, A. (1992). *Historical Anthropology of the Middle Ages* (Chicago).

Hagedorn, D. (1985). "Zum Amt des διοικητής im römischen Aegypten," *Yale Classical Studies* 28: 167–210.

Hanson, A. E. (1989). "Village officials at Philadelphia: a model of Romanization in the Julio-Claudian period," *Egitto e storia antica dall'ellenismo all'età araba. Bilancio di un confronto*, ed. L. Criscuolo and G. Geraci (Bologna) 429–40.

Harris, W. V. (1989). *Ancient Literacy* (Cambridge, Mass.).

Herlihy, D. and Klapisch-Zuber, C. (1985). *Tuscans and their Families: A Study of the Florentine Catasto of 1427* (New Haven).

Hobson, D. W. (1983). "Women as property owners in Roman Egypt," *Transactions of the American Philological Association* 113: 311–21.

—— (1984a). "The role of women in the economic life of Roman Egypt: a case study from first century Tebtunis," *Echos du Monde Classique/Classical Views* 28 = n.s. 3: 373–90.

—— (1984b). "Agricultural land and economic life in Soknopaiou Nesos," *BASP* 21: 89–109.

—— (1988). "Towards a broader context of the study of Greco-Roman Egypt," *Echos du Monde Classique/Classical Views* 32 = n.s. 7: 353–63.

—— (1989). "Naming practices in Roman Egypt," *BASP* 26: 157–74.

Husson, G. (1979). "L'habitat monastique en Égypte," *Hommages à la mémoire de Serge Sauneron* II (Bd'E 82, Cairo) 191–207.

—— (1983). *OIKIA. Le vocabulaire de la maison privée en Égypte d'après les papyrus grecs* (Paris).

Jones, A. H. M. (1964). *The Later Roman Empire* (Oxford).

Katzoff, R. (1985). "*Donatio ante nuptias* and Jewish Dowry Additions," *Yale Classical Studies* 28: 231–44.

Keenan, J. G. (1975). "On law and society in late Roman Egypt," *ZPE* 17: 237–50.
—— (1980). "Aurelius Phoibammon, son of Triadelphus: a Byzantine Egyptian land entrepreneur," *BASP* 17: 145–54.
—— (1985). "Village shepherds and social tension in Byzantine Egypt," *Yale Classical Studies* 28: 245–59.
—— (1989). "Pastoralism in Roman Egypt," *BASP* 26: 175–200.
—— (1991). "The 'new papyrology' and ancient social history," *Ancient History Bulletin* 5: 159–69.
—— (1992). "A Constantinople loan, AD 541," *BASP* 29: 175–82.
—— (1993). "Papyrology and Byzantine history," *BASP* 30: 137–44.
Kehoe, D. P. (1992). *Management and Investment on Estates in Roman Egypt during the Early Empire* (Bonn).
Koenen, L. (1975). "Ein Mönch als Berufsschreiber. Zur Buchproduktion im 5./6. Jahrhundert," *Festschrift zum 150jährigen Bestehen des Berliner Ägyptischen Museums* (Berlin) 347–54.
Le Goff, J. and Nora, P. (1985). *Constructing the Past, Essays in Historical Methodology* (Cambridge).
Le Roy Ladurie, E. (1981). *The Mind and Method of the Historian* (Chicago).
Lewis, D. M. (1994). "The Persepolis tablets: speech, seal and script," in Bowman and Woolf (1994) 17–32.
Lewis, N. (1970). "Greco-Roman Egypt: fact or fiction," *Proceedings of the XII International Congress of Papyrology* (Am Stud. Pap. 7; Toronto) 3–14.
—— (1974). *Papyrus in Classical Antiquity.* (Oxford).
—— (1981). "Literati in the service of Roman emperors: politics before culture," *Coins, Culture, and History in the Ancient World: Numismatic and Other Studies in Honor of Bluma L. Trell* (Detroit) 149–66.
—— (1984). "The Romanity of Roman Egypt: a growing consensus," *Atti del XVII Congresso Internazionale di Papirologia* (Naples) III 1077–84.
—— (1989). *Papyrus in Classical Antiquity. A Supplement* (Papyrologica Bruxellensia 23, Brussels).
—— (1993). "The demise of the Demotic document: when and why," *Journal of Egyptian Archaeology* 79: 276–81.
MacCoull, L. S. B. (1992). "Towards an appropriate context for the study of late antique Egypt," *Ancient History Bulletin* 6.2 (1992) 73–9.
—— (forthcoming). "A new look at the career of John Philoponus," *Journal of Early Christian Studies.*
Maddern, P. C. (1992). *Violence and Social Order, East Anglia 1422–1442* (Oxford).
Martin, A. (1994). "Archives privées et cachettes documentaires," *Proceedings of the 20th International Congress of Papyrologists* (Copenhagen) 569–77.
Martin, R. (1989). *The Past Within Us: An Empirical Approach to Philosophy of History* (Princeton).
Mélèze-Modrzejewski, J. (1988). "'La loi des Égyptiens:' le droit grec

dans l'Égypte romaine," *Proceedings of the XVIII International Congress of Papyrology* (Athens) II: 383–99; reprinted in the author's *Droit impérial et traditions locales dans l'Égypte romaine* (Aldershot 1990), ch. IX.

Merton, R. K. (1967). *On Theoretical Sociology. Five Essays Old and New* (New York).

Montevecchi, O. (1973, 1988²). *La papirologia* (Turin/Milan).

Morris, I. (1994). "The Athenian economy twenty years after *The Ancient Economy*," *CP* 89: 351–66.

Orrieux, C. (1983). *Les papyrus de Zénon: L'horizon d'un grec en Égypte au IIIe siècle avant J. C.* (Paris).

—— (1985). *Zénon de Caunos, parépidèmos, et le destin grec* (Paris).

Paglagean, E. (1977). *Pauvreté économique et pauvreté sociale à Byzance, IVe-VIIe siècle* (Paris).

Palmer, B. D. (1990). *Descent into Discourse. The Reification of Language and the Writing of Social History* (Philadelphia).

Papini, L. (1983). "Notes on the formulary of some Coptic documentary papyri from Middle Egypt," *Bulletin de la Société d'Archéologie Copte* 25: 83–9.

Parkin, T. G. (1992). *Demography and Roman Society* (Baltimore).

Parsons, P. J. (1967). "Philippus Arabs and Egypt," *JRS* 57: 134–41.

—— (1980). "Background: the papyrus letter," *Acta Colloquii Didactici Classici Octavi = Didactica Classica Gandensia* 20: 3–18.

—— (1994). "Summing up," *Proceedings of the 20th International Congress of Papyrologists* (Copenhagen) 118–23.

Peremans, W. and van 't Dack, E. (1979). "Papyrologie et histoire ancienne," *Actes du XVe Congrès International de Papyrologie* (Brussels) 4: 7–25.

Pestman, P. W. (1978). "L'agoranomie: un avant-poste de l'administration grecque enlevé par les Égyptiens?" *Das Ptolemäische Aegypten*, ed. V. M. Strocka and H. Maehler (Mainz) 203–10.

—— (1992). *Il processo di Hermias e altri documenti dell'archivio dei Choachiti (P. Tor. Choachiti)* (Catalogo del Museo Egizio di Torino, 1 ser., Monumenti e Testi, 6; Turin).

Peterman, G. L. (1993). "The Petra scrolls," *ACOR Newsletter* 5.2: 1–3.

Pomeroy, S. B. (1986). "Copronyms and the exposure of infants in papyri," *Studies in Roman Law in Memory of A. Arthur Schiller* (Leiden) 147–62.

Préaux, C. (1939). *L'économie royale des Lagides* (Brussels).

—— (1959). "Papyrologie et sociologie," *Annales Universitatis Saraviensis* 8: 5–20.

Preisendanz, K. (1933). *Papyrusfunde und Papyrusforschung* (Leipzig).

Quaegebeur, J. (1989). "The Egyptian clergy and the cult of the Ptolemaic dynasty," *Ancient Society* 20: 93–116.

Rathbone, D. (1989). "The ancient economy and Graeco-Roman Egypt," *Egitto e storia antica dall'Ellenismo all'età araba. Bilancio di un confronto*, ed. Lucia Criscuolo and G. Geraci (Bologna) 159–76.

—— (1991). *Economic Rationalism and Rural Society in Third-Century AD*

Egypt: The Heroninos Archive and the Appianus Estate (Cambridge).

Ray, J. D. (1994). "Literacy and language in Egypt in the late and Persian periods," in Bowman and Woolf (1994) 51–66.

Rémondon, R. (1964). "Problèmes de bilinguisme dans l'Égypte lagide (U.P.Z. I, 148)," *Chronique d'Égypte* 39: 126–46.

Robert, L. (1961). "L'épigraphie", *L'histoire et ses méthodes*, ed. Ch. Samaran (Encyclopédie de la Pléiade; Paris) 453–97 = *Die Epigraphik der klassischen Welt* (Bonn 1970).

Rostovtzeff, M. I. (1922). *A Large Estate in Egypt in the Third Century B.C.* (Madison).

—— (1941). *Social and Economic History of the Hellenistic World* (Oxford).

Rupprecht, H.-A. (1994). *Kleine Einführung in die Papyruskunde* (Darmstadt).

Schuman, V. B. (1972). "An archive in the Old Style," *BASP* 9: 71–84.

Scott, J. C. (1985). *Weapons of the Weak: Everyday Forms of Peasant Resistance* (New Haven).

Sharpe, J. L. (1992). "The Dakhleh tablets and some codicological considerations," *Les tablettes d'écrire de l'antiquité a l'époque moderne*, ed. E. Lalou (Turnhout) 127–48.

Sheridan, J. A. (1995). *Columbia Papyri* IX (Atlanta).

Sijpesteijn, P. J. and Worp, K. A. (1978). *Zwei Landlisten aus dem Hermupolites (P. Landlisten)* (Stud. Amst. 7; Zutphen).

Skeat, T. C. (1982). "The length of the standard papyrus roll and the cost-advantage of the codex," *ZPE* 45: 169–75.

Stock, B. (1990). *Listening for the Text. On the Uses of the Past* (Baltimore).

Stone, L. (1994). Lecture for 1985 in D. Greenberg and S. N. Katz, eds., *The Life of Learning* (New York 1994).

Thomas, J. D. (1975). "The introduction of dekaprotoi and comarchs into Egypt in the third century AD," *ZPE* 19: 111–19.

Thompson, D. J. (1988). *Memphis Under the Ptolemies* (Princeton).

—— (1994). "Literacy and power in Ptolemaic Egypt," in Bowman and Woolf (1994) 67–83.

Török, L. (1988). *Late Antique Nubia* (Budapest).

Turner, E. G. (1968, 1980²). *Greek Papyri: An Introduction* (Oxford).

—— (1973). *The Papyrologist at Work* (Durham, N.C.).

Van Minnen, P. (1986a). "A change of names in Roman Egypt after AD 202? A Note on P.Amst. I 72," *ZPE* 62: 87–92.

—— (1986b). "The volume of the Oxyrhynchite textile trade," *Münstersche Beiträge zur Antiken Handelsgeschichte* 5.2: 88–95.

—— (1993). "The century of papyrology (1892–1992)," *BASP* 30: 5–18.

—— (1994). "House to house enquiries: an interdisciplinary approach to Roman Karanis," *ZPE* 100: 227–51.

—— and Worp, K. A. (1993). "The Greek and Latin Literary Texts from Hermopolis," *GRBS* 34: 151–86.

Wagner, G. (1987). *Les oasis d'Égypte à l'époque grecque, romaine et byzantine d'après les documents grecs (Recherches de papyrologie et d'épigraphie grecques)* (Bd'E 100, Cairo).

Will, E. (1985). "Pour une 'anthropologie coloniale' du monde
hellénistique," *The Craft of the Ancient Historian. Essays in Honor of
Chester G. Starr,* ed. J. W. Eadie and J. Ober (Lanham) 273–301.

Wipszycka, E. (1986). "La valeur de l'onomastique pour l'histoire de
la christianisation de l'Égypte," *ZPE* 62: 173–81.

—— (1988). "La christianisation de l'Égypte aux IVᵉ–VIᵉ siècles.
Aspects sociaux et ethniques," *Aegyptus* 68: 119–65.

—— (1993). "Les ordres mineurs dans l'Eglise d'Égypte du IVᵉ au
VIIIᵉ siècle," *Journal of Juristic Papyrology* 23: 181–215.

—— (1994). "Le monachisme égyptien et les villes," *Travaux et
Mémoires* 12: 1–44.

Woolf, G. (1994). "Power and the spread of writing in the West," in
Bowman and Woolf (1994) 84–98.

Youtie, H. C. (1963). "The papyrologist: artificer of fact," *GRBS* 4:
19–32 (= *Scriptiunculae* I [Amsterdam 1973] 9–23).

—— (1966a). "Pétaus, fils de Pétaus, ou le scribe qui ne savait pas
écrire," *Chronique d'Égypte* 41: 127–43 (= *Scriptiunculae* II [Amster-
dam 1973] 677–93).

—— (1966b). "Text and context in transcribing papyri," *GRBS* 7:
251–8 (= *Scriptiunculae* I [Amsterdam] 25–33).

—— (1970). "Callimachus in the tax rolls," *Proceedings of the Twelfth
International Congress of Papyrology* (Toronto) 545–51.

—— (1974²). *The Textual Criticism of Documentary Papyri* (London).

Yoyotte, J. (1969). "Bakhtis: religion égyptienne et culture grecque à
Edfou," *Religions en Égypte hellénistique et romaine* (Paris) 127–41.

General bibliography

The literature of papyrology is vast. This highly selective bibliography steers the student primarily to reference works through which more information can be found; it is limited to works in the principal western scholarly languages. A very extensive, up-to-date, well-organized, and carefully chosen bibliography can be found in the new manual of H.-A. Rupprecht (no. I.5 below).

I. INTRODUCTORY WORKS

1 E. G. Turner, *Greek Papyri* (Oxford 1968; 2nd ed. 1980), the only useful general work in English; emphasis on literary papyri.
2 P. W. Pestman, *The New Papyrological Primer* (Leiden 1990), a selection of texts with notes (but no translations) and a general introduction.
3 O. Montevecchi, *La papirologia* (Turin 1973; 2nd ed. Milan 1988), large in scope and scale, with massive (but poorly organized) bibliographies.
4 A. Bataille, *Les papyrus* (Traité d'études byzantines 2, Paris 1955).
5 H.-A. Rupprecht, *Kleine Einführung in die Papyruskunde* (Darmstadt 1994).
6 I. Gallo, *Greek and Latin Papyrology* (London 1986).

II. BIBLIOGRAPHICAL GUIDES

1 *Bibliographie Papyrologique*, published on disk and paper four times per year (Fondation Égyptologique Reine Elisabeth, Brussels); electronic version for 1976–94 available from Scholars Press (Atlanta).
2 J. F. Oates, R. S. Bagnall, W. H. Willis and K. A. Worp, *Checklist of Editions of Greek and Latin Papyri, Ostraca and Tablets* (4th ed. Atlanta 1992; electronic version with Duke Data Bank of Documentary Papyri on Packard Humanities Institute CD-ROM): list of standard

abbreviations of papyri, ostraka, tablets, corpora, series, papyrological congresses, reference tools and journals with full bibliographic information.
3 S. P. Vleeming and A. A. den Brinker, *Check-list of Demotic Text Editions and Re-editions* (Leiden 1993). Includes a listing of re-editions of individual texts.
4 A. A. Schiller, "Checklist of editions of Coptic documents and letters," *BASP* 13 (1976) 99–123.
5 *Aegyptus* (Milan, annual) includes a listing of newly published texts and a classified bibliography.
6 "Chronique: Égypte gréco-romaine et monde hellénistique," by J. Mélèze-Modrzejewski, periodically in *Revue historique de droit français et étranger* (Paris). Summaries and some critical remarks, concentrated on law but with a broad reach.
7 H.-J. Thissen, "Demotische Literaturübersicht," in each volume of *Enchoria*; 18 reports through 1991.
8 T. Orlandi, *Coptic Bibliography* (Rome 1989–).
9 T. G. Wilfong, "Western Thebes in the seventh and eighth centuries: a bibliographic survey of Jême and its surroundings," *BASP* 26 (1989) 89–145.
10 R. Pack, *Index of Greek and Latin Literary Texts from Greco-Roman Egypt* (2nd ed. Ann Arbor 1965), a fundamental listing of literary papyri with full references; now much out of date, 3rd ed. in preparation by P. Mertens.
11 J. van Haelst, *Catalogue des papyrus littéraires juifs et chrétiens* (Paris 1976).
12 F. Preisigke *et al.*, *Berichtigungsliste der griechischen Papyrusurkunden* (1913–), 8 vols. to date plus one index vol., continuing. A systematic listing of corrections and reeditions of documentary papyri.

III. PAPYRUS AND PALAEOGRAPHY

1 N. Lewis, *Papyrus in Classical Antiquity* (Oxford 1973); *A Supplement* (Brussels 1989).
2 F. G. Kenyon, *Books and Readers* (Oxford 1951).
3 W. Schubart, *Das Buch bei den Griechen und Römern* (2nd ed. Berlin 1921).
4 E. G. Turner, *Greek Manuscripts of the Ancient World* (2nd ed. by P. J. Parsons, London 1987).
5 W. Schubart, *Griechische Paläographie* (Handbuch d. Altert., Munich 1925).
6 Cl. Préaux, "Sur l'écriture des ostraca thébains d'époque romaine," *Journal of Egyptian Archaeology* 40 (1954) 83–87, a brilliant study of the handwriting of ostraka.
7 C. H. Roberts, *Manuscript, Society and Belief in Early Christian Egypt* (London 1979).

IV. COLLECTIONS OF PAPYRI

1 F. Preisigke *et al.*, *Sammelbuch griechischer Urkunden aus Aegypten* (1915–), 18 vols. to date; reprints texts of papyri etc. published in journals or short, unindexed publications; provides index.
2 Duke Data Bank of Documentary Papyri, CD-ROM published by Packard Humanities Institute. Current version contains full texts of all papyri published from 1932 to the present in searchable form.
3 L. Mitteis and U. Wilcken, *Grundzüge und Chrestomathie der Papyruskunde* (Leipzig 1912): 2 vols. of introduction, 2 of selected texts, one pair each for history and law. Still the fundamental introduction to documents.
4 C. C. Edgar and A. S. Hunt, *Select Papyri* (Loeb Classical Library, Cambridge, Mass./London 1932–34), 2 vols. of non-literary papyri.
5 D. L. Page, *Select Papyri* (Loeb Classical Library, Cambridge, Mass./ London 1941), poetic texts only.

V. COLLECTIONS ON SPECIFIC SUBJECTS

1 M.-Th. Lenger, *Corpus des ordonnances des Ptolémées* (2nd ed. Brussels 1980; supplement Brussels 1990): Ptolemaic legislation.
2 P. M. Meyer, *Juristische Papyri* (Berlin 1920).
3 V. Arangio-Rùiz, *Fontes Iuris Romani Anteiustiniani* III (Florence 1943).
4 V. Tcherikover and A. Fuks, *Corpus Papyrorum Judaicarum* (Cambridge, Mass. 1957–64), 3 vols.
5 R. Cavenaile, *Corpus Papyrorum Latinarum* (Wiesbaden 1956).
6 S. Daris, *Documenti per la storia dell'esercito romano in Egitto* (Milan 1964).
7 R. O. Fink, *Roman Military Records on Papyrus* (Cleveland 1971).

VI. COLLECTIONS OF PLATES (SEE ALSO SECTION III ABOVE)

1 Montevecchi (no. 1.3) has a list of published plates of securely datable papyri arranged by year, very useful.
2 W. Schubart, *Papyri Graecae Berolinenses* (Bonn 1911).
3 M. Norsa, *La scrittura letteraria greca* (Pisa 1939).
4 M. Norsa, *Papiri greci delle collezioni italiane, scritture documentarie* (Pisa 1946), 3 parts.
5 C. H. Roberts, *Greek Literary Hands* (Oxford 1956).
6 R. Seider, *Paläographie der griechischen Papyri* (Stuttgart 1967–).
7 E. Boswinkel and P. J. Sijpesteijn, *Greek Papyri, Ostraca, and Mummy Labels* (Amsterdam 1968).
8 G. Cavallo and H. Maehler, *Greek Bookhands of the Early Byzantine Period AD 300–800* (London 1987).
9 Of published volumes of papyri with plates, see especially *P.Lond.*, Atlas I–III; *P.Mert.* I–II; *P.Amh.* II; *P.Ryl.* I–IV; *CPR* V–XVIII.

VII. REFERENCE WORKS ON THE LANGUAGES OF THE PAPYRI

1 F. Preisigke *et al.*, *Wörterbuch der griechischen Papyrusurkunden* (1924–). Vols. I–II, dictionary; vol. III, special lists of kings, officials, taxes, etc.; vol. IV, a supplement in form of dictionary, 5 fasc. to date (through zeta). Suppl. I (1969–71) in 3 parts gives references only for texts published 1941–66. Suppl. II (1991) does the same for texts published 1967–1976.
2 F. Preisigke, *Namenbuch* (Heidelberg 1922): index of names in papyri etc.
3 D. Foraboschi, *Onomasticon Alterum Papyrologicum* (Milan 1967–71), supplements the preceding up to about 1965.
4 E. Mayser, *Grammatik der griechischen Papyri der Ptolemäerzeit* (1906–), 2 vols. in several parts; revision by H. Schmoll continues irregularly.
5 Liddell and Scott, *Greek Lexicon* with 1968 *Supplement* has a considerable amount of papyrological material, but is selective and often peculiar.
6 F. T. Gignac, *A Grammar of the Non-literary Papyri of the Roman and Byzantine Periods* (Milan 1976–), 2 vols. to date (Phonology, Morphology).
7 H. C. Youtie, *Textual Criticism of Documentary Papyri* (2nd ed. London 1974)
8 E. Lüddeckens *et al.*, *Demotisches Namenbuch* (Wiesbaden 1980–), in progress, 12 fascicles to date.
9 W. Erichsen, *Demotisches Glossar* (Copenhagen 1954).
10 W. E. Crum, *A Coptic Dictionary* (Oxford 1939).

VIII. PROSOPOGRAPHIES

1 W. Peremans, E. van 't Dack *et al.*, *Prosopographia Ptolemaica* (Louvain 1950–), 9 vols. to date, arranged systematically.
2 G. Bastianini and J. Whitehorne, *Strategi and Royal Scribes of Roman Egypt* (Florence 1987).
3 J. M. Diethart, *Prosopographia Arsinoitica* I (Vienna 1980), covering the sixth to eighth centuries.
4 B. Jones and J. Whitehorne, *Register of Oxyrhynchites* (Chico 1980), covering 30 BC to AD 96.

IX. CHRONOLOGY

1 T. C. Skeat, *The Reigns of the Ptolemies* (Munich 1954, 2 ed. 1969).
2 A. E. Samuel, *Ptolemaic Chronology* (Munich 1962).
3 P. W. Pestman, *Chronologie égyptienne* (Leiden 1965).
4 P. Bureth, *Les titulatures impériales* (Brussels 1964).
5 R. S. Bagnall and K. A. Worp, *Chronological Systems of Byzantine Egypt* (Zutphen 1978).

6 R. S. Bagnall and K. A. Worp, *Regnal Formulas in Byzantine Egypt* (Missoula 1979).
7 T. C. Skeat, *The Reign of Augustus in Egypt* (Munich 1993).
8 R. S. Bagnall, A. Cameron, S. Schwartz and K. A. Worp, *Consuls of the Later Roman Empire* (Atlanta 1987).

X. SOME GUIDES TO RECENT LITERATURE

1 R. S. Bagnall, "Papyrology and Ptolemaic history, 1956–1980," *Classical World* 76 (1982–83) 13–21.
2 R. S. Bagnall, "Archaeology and papyrology," *Journal of Roman Archaeology* 1 (1988) 197–202.
3 A. K. Bowman, "Papyri and Roman imperial history: 1960–75," *Journal of Roman Studies* 66 (1976) 153–73.
4 J. G. Keenan, "Papyrology and Roman history, 1956–80," *Classical World* 76 (1982) 23–31.

Index